D1134400

GALLIPOLI
1915

EXPLORE HISTORY'S MAJOR CONFLICTS
WITH BATTLE STORY

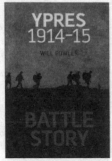

GALLIPOLI
1915

PETER DOYLE

To the lads they left behind

First published 2011
by Spellmount, an imprint of
The History Press
The Mill, Brimscombe Port
Stroud, Gloucestershire, GL5 2QG
www.thehistorypress.co.uk

British Library Cataloguing in Publication Data.
A catalogue record for this book is available from the British Library.

ISBN 978 0 7524 6310 0

Typesetting and origination by The History Press
Printed in Malta
Manufacturing managed by Jellyfish Print Solutions Ltd

CONTENTS

ACKNOWLEDGEMENTS

I would like to thank a range of friends and colleagues who have helped inform my ideas on the Gallipoli campaign: Kenan Çelik, Peter Chasseaud, Ashley Ekins, Peter Hart, Savas Karaças, Bill Sellars and Nigel Steel – and to Chris Malone for the chance to explore my ideas during the making of the the TV documentary *Battlefield Detectives: Gallipoli*. I am grateful for the Trustees of the Imperial War Museum for granting me access to the material in their magnificent archive, and to the National Archives in Kew. The richness of the writing that surrounds the campaign should also be celebrated. Other than those I've taken or that are from my collection, the illustrations are gathered from the pictorial publications of the day, particularly important are *The War Illustrated* (Amalgamated Press) and *The Illustrated War News*. I am also grateful for access to the free online resources of the Great War Picture Archive, Wikimedia Commons and the Library of Congress. Gallipoli is a special place, both beautiful and tragic: I am glad that I have been able to share it with my fellow battlefield travellers, Julie and James.

LIST OF ILLUSTRATIONS

17 Men of the Australian and New Zealand Army Corps training at Giza.

18 Australian Field battery in action at Gallipoli.

19 The Gallipoli Star intended for all members of the Australian and New Zealand Army Corps, but was not awarded.

20 General William Birdwood.

21 The epitome of Anzac spirit; an Australian sergeant.

22 French colonial troops.

23 Medaille d'Orient.

24 General Gourard, commander of the Corps Expeditionaire d'Orient.

25 French infantryman carries a wounded comrade in Gallipoli.

26 Map of the Gallipoli Peninsula, showing the main fortresses.

27 The fleet steams into the Dardanelles.

28 HMS *Irresistible*.

29 Destroyed gun at Fort No. I (Etrugrul).

30 Modern satellite view of the Dardanelles and the Gallipoli Peninsula.

31 'The Sphinx'.

32 Achi Baba.

33 The Helles Front, showing the main landing beaches.

34 Major General Sir Aylmer Hunter-Weston.

35 The assault on V Beach from the SS *River Clyde*.

36 An analysis of V Beach.

37 Captain Willis leads the Lancashire Fusiliers at W Beach.

38 Map of the Anzac sector.

39 Anzac Cove.

40 Steele's Post.

41 HMS *Majestic*, sunk off Cape Helles.

42 A charge by the Royal Naval Division, Third Battle of Krithia.

43 Anzacs at work making jam tin bombs.

44 Periscope rifle, one of many devices invented in Gallipoli.

List of Illustrations

Front cover: Turkish soldiers firing from Halil Bey Hill toward Gelik Lake, courtesy of General Staff Archives, Ankara.

INTRODUCTION

When the moon shines bright on Charlie Chaplin,
He's going balmy
To join the Army;
And his old baggy trousers want a-mending
Before they send him
To the Dardanelles

Gallipoli – almost 100 years on and the name of this ill-fated campaign still resonates. Historians are divided: was this brief campaign, fought from April 1915 to January 1916, doomed from the start, a hopeless endeavour that was guaranteed to do nothing other than preside over the tragic slaughter of its protagonists? Or was it a bold step, a masterful stroke of genius that was to become bogged down as momentum was lost and trench warfare took over? Certainly the German Commander, Liman von Sanders, believed it could have succeeded, but as the years have passed opinions have become more divided.

Forgotten, more often than not, is the fact that this was an Ottoman victory. And not just a victory by default, but a resounding victory that saw the Allies hemmed into three small fragments of the Peninsula, unable to breakout. With tenacious soldiery under skilful leadership (only a few of whom were German), intelligent use of terrain and husbanding of resources on home territory by the Ottoman forces, the Allies had little choice but to leave the Peninsula and depart, Constantinople never under threat. For these reasons, Çanakkale is rightly remembered in modern Turkey.

In recent years, Gallipoli has become a battleground of a new sort, a war of words between nationalities seeking to apportion blame for what was ultimately a failure. Recriminations commenced before the campaign was over; reputations were destroyed. Winston Churchill was to fall from grace, and would serve his own time on the Western Front as a battalion commander. General Sir Ian Hamilton, Commander-in-Chief of the military forces, an Edwardian gentleman and one of Britain's most senior and experienced soldiers, would never again serve in a meaningful military capacity. Like Vimy Ridge for the Canadians, Gallipoli has also become associated with the birth of nationhood – with the emergence of Australia and New Zealand from behind the skirts of the mother country, and of the rising of the new nation of Turkey from the burning embers of the Ottoman Empire.

Over the last 25 years there has been an increase in the numbers of people visiting Gallipoli. For Turks, the campaign was a well-executed defence of their homeland, and this has led to an increased memorialisation of the Peninsula that has proceeded apace – in line, in fact, with the increased interest in attending the Dawn Service, predominantly a remembrance of the landings at Anzac Cove on 25 April 1915. Every year, thousands of people from Australia and New Zealand flock to the small cove that was officially named Anzac by Mustafa Kemal Atatürk, former military commander and future father of his new country. This has created tensions, as the great mass of people struggle with the limited facilities, unintentionally causing decay and erosion of the fragile surfaces, and leading, controversially, to a new roadway that cut through the fragile battlefield terrain, exposing, according to some sources, the bleached white bones of supposed soldiers' remains. Perhaps understandably, each new generation sees the campaign as a struggle of ANZAC soldiers (and therein, mostly Australians) with the Turks, led hopelessly by ineffectual British generals. As with all military history, the truth is somewhat more complex.

The campaign at Gallipoli in 1915 was short – operated over just eight months – and was exceptionally bloody. Casualties were high, as were deaths and debilitating illnesses from disease and poor hygiene. Logistically difficult and poorly planned, Gallipolli was to serve as a perfect example of how not to carry out an amphibious landing. Without Gallipoli the planning for the Normandy landings in 1944 would have been a lot more difficult, its lessons studied by military academies worldwide.

Contentious, very many books have been published that tread the well-worn path of discussing the campaign, considering its what-ifs, and drawing conclusions based on its stated aims. There have been accounts from each of the protagonists (though relatively little accessible work from the Ottoman side), from the soldiers themselves, and treatises that have examined the minutiae of the campaign from its mapping through to its medical preparations. There has been much original research and many new angles. This book is necessarily a summary of much of this scholarship, and is intended as a brief overview of some of the most important aspects. It is meant to act as a basic introduction to the campaign for a new audience. Though truly an all-arm combined amphibious operation – the largest such endeavour carried out at this point – the focus of the book is the military campaign, rather than the naval prelude.

Throughout this book, the spellings and names are as used by the Allies at the time; the terms 'the Straits' and 'the Dardanelles' are used interchangeably (the term Narrows restricted only to that point between Chanak – modern Çanakkale, and Maidos – modern Eceabat). I have used the term 'Allies' to encompass both what are strictly the 'Entente' Powers (Britain, France and Russia), and also the Imperial forces of France and Britain – from Senegal, Australia, New Zealand, India – and, at its later stage, Newfoundland.

TIMELINE

Gallipoli 1915

1915

25 February	Second naval attack on the Dardanelles defences
13 March	General Sir Ian Hamilton appointed to command the Mediterranean Expeditionary Force (MEF)
13 March	Commodore Roger Keyes leads night minesweeping operation
16 March	Admiral Carden resigns, Vice-Admiral de Robeck takes charge of naval operations
18 March	Naval attempt to force the Dardanelles fails, with the loss of three battleships sunk by mines, and four others badly damaged
22 March	Decision taken to land at Dardanelles by Hamilton and de Robeck
25 April	Battles of the Beaches commence; British 29th Division at Cape Helles, Anzac Corps at Ari Burnu, French Corps Expeditionaire d'Orient at Kum Kale
27 April	Ottomans counterattack in Anzac sector
28 April	First Battle of Krithia: 3,000 British and French casualties
6–8 May	Second Battle of Krithia commences, 42nd East Lancashire Division lands
12–13 May	Australian Light Horse Brigade and New Zealand Mounted Rifles Brigade land at Anzac Beach as reinforcements
18 May	Large Ottoman attack at Anzac Beach: 10,000 Ottoman casualties
4 June	Third Battle of Krithia
28 June–5 July	Battle of Gully Ravine
12 July	British 52nd (Lowland) Division and Royal Naval Division (RND) attack at Achi Baba Nullah
6 August	Major Allied offensive commences

Timeline

1915	6 August	Suvla Bay landings commence, General Frederick Stopford commanding
	6–12 August	Battle of Lone Pine by Australian 1st Division
	6–13 August	Battle of the Vineyard (Helles sector), by British 29th Division
	7 August	Attack of the 3rd Light Horse at the Nek with heavy losses
	8–10 August	Battle of Chunuk Bair, attack by New Zealand and British forces repulsed by Mustafa Kemal
	15 August	General Sir Frederick Stopford replaced as commander of IX Corps
	21–29 August	Battle of Hill 60, Suvla sector
	19 September	1st Newfoundland Regiment arrives as reinforcements, to serve in the 29th Division
	15 October	General Hamilton relieved of command
	28 October	General Sir Charles Monro assumes command of the MEF
	15 November	Field Marshal Kitchener visits Gallipoli, recommending evacuation seven days later
	27 November	Blizzard conditions on the Peninsula
	7 December	Evacuation of Anzac and Suvla ordered
	19–20 December	Anzac sector and Suvla Bay evacuated
	28 December	Evacuation of Helles sector ordered
1916	7 January	Ottoman assault along Gully Spur, Helles sector
	8–9 January	Cape Helles evacuated

HISTORICAL BACKGROUND

The Balkans had seen an almost constant state of unrest since the end of the Crimean War. The volatility of the region was in part due to the parlous state of two of the oldest empires, the Austro-Hungarian Empire of the Hapsburgs and the Ottoman Empire, the 'Sick Old Man of Europe'. Riven by ethnic differences and the birth of new national awareness, the Balkan states turned inwards on each other in 1912–13, creating a powder keg that would ultimately lead to the outbreak of the First World War almost exactly a year later, and a headlong rush into conflict. Within weeks of the assassination of the Archduke Franz Ferdinand in Sarajevo on 28 June 1914, the major European powers were at each other's throats, with, according to British Foreign Minister Sir Edward Grey, 'the lights going out all over Europe'.

For the Ottoman Empire, the prospect of another war after those fought in 1912–13 was an unpalatable one. Though the Young Turks who had overthrown the Sultan in 1909 had set about modernising the country and the military, it had been inadequate. The Ottomans had been roundly beaten in the Balkan Wars, its European possessions stripped bare to a small component of Thrace and that sliver of land that was to form the northern shore of the Dardanelles, the ancient Hellespont that had fascinated classicists for decades.

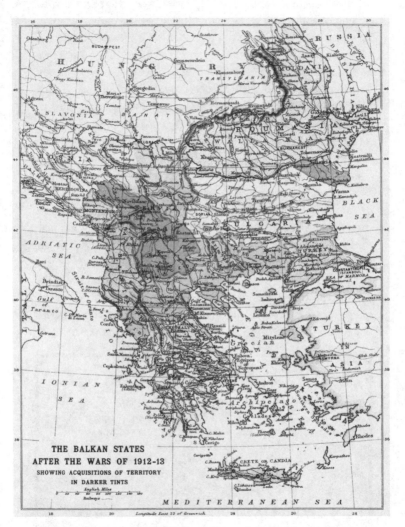

1. The Balkan States. The Balkan Wars of 1912–13 were to have devastating results for the Ottomans, already under pressure in North Africa. After losing the First Balkan War, most of the Ottoman territory in Europe would be severely curtailed.

The Dardanelles, a narrow passageway between European and Asian Turkey, is a tightly constrained waterway that was created by geological faulting over millennia. This strategic waterway connects the Aegean Sea and Mediterranean with the Sea of Marmara and ultimately, through the Bosphorus, to the Black Sea, and had been a point of interest to military minds for centuries. Constantinople, (now the modern city of Istanbul), sits astride the Bosphorus and guards the entrance to the Black Sea, thereby controlling entry to the winter ports of Russia. Because of this and a myriad of other reasons, Constantinople had been coveted for centuries, particularly by the old enemies of Greece and Russia.

In European Turkey, the shores of the Dardanelles are guarded by the Gallipoli Peninsula, a narrow finger of land named after its principal settlement (Gelibolu, or Gallipoli). Opposing this is the Asiatic shore, the Aegean expression of the great Anatolian Peninsula, the greater part of modern Turkey, and the heart of the ailing Ottoman Empire in 1915. Fortified for centuries, the idea of squeezing a fleet of ships between the beetling brows of the shores of the Dardanelles had exercised the mind of the military of many nations for centuries, particularly so in the complex diplomacies of two centuries before the Gallipoli landings of 1915.

THE YOUNG TURKS

At the close of the nineteenth century, the Young Turks had grown as a movement from groups of dissident university students to a national movement – the Committee of Union and Progress, committed to a regime in which the Sultanate was a constitutional monarchy. In 1907, militant members of the Ottoman Freedom Society raised by Mehmet Talat worked under the umbrella of the CUP. The militant nationalists would become powerful; one of them, Ismal Enver, became Secretary of State for War, and would face significant challenges in 1914–15; another was Mustafa Kemal.

2. *Constantinople from the Bosphorus; Allied hopes were pinned on the Ottoman capital faltering if the fleet got through the Straits.*

When war with Germany was declared on 4 August 1914, the Ottoman Empire ostensibly remained neutral; yet already the Ottomans had signed a treaty with Germany that would bind them into the Central Powers. For the Kaiser, the possibility of a Greater Germany, and an influence that would spread through the Balkans and into the Middle East, was an unbridled dream that would manifest itself in the construction of an unbroken railway link from Berlin to Baghdad, through Thracian Turkey and into Anatolia, passing over the Bosphorus at Constantinople. This would pass through aligned nations, with Bulgaria and the Ottoman Empire pivotal in this; it was inconvenient, though, that belligerent Serbia sat squarely in the way.

Germany was also keen to ensure that its eastern enemy, Russia, was depleted in both supplies and support. As most Russian war materiel would have to travel, on the southern, winter, route through the Straits and into the Black Sea, the temptation to make certain that the Dardanelles was closed to traffic was pressing. German influence was already strong, with military missions to the Ottomans from the late nineteenth century; it was to grow when, on 3 August 1914, the British clumsily requisitioned two warships being built in

British shipyards, at great cost to the Ottoman populace. Tensions came to a head on 10 August, when the German warships *Goeben* and *Breslau* were granted passage through the technically neutral Dardanelles to Constantinople, to become symbolic substitutes for the ships 'stolen' by the British. A final blow to British influence was the appointment of the German Admiral Souchon to the command of the Ottoman Navy – the *Goeben* and *Breslau* now technically Ottoman ships, the *Yazus Sultan Salim* and the *Midilli*.

With the Ottomans committed to war, some means was sought to make sure that they would be quickly despatched; for the British and French this would remove the possibility of Ottoman belligerency against their possessions and protectorates in the Middle East. Both had low opinions of the Ottoman military – defeat in the last Balkan War in 1913 was surely indicative of what might be expected in the coming conflict. But how would this be achieved? There were other players in the arena.

For centuries there had been Greek and Russian aspirations to possess the Imperial city of Constantinople, sitting astride the Bosphorus and in ultimate control of the Black Sea route. With the Ottomans in an uncertain period, the gears of diplomacy started to grind – the essential goal was the carving up of what remained of the Ottoman Empire, spreading from European Thrace into the Arabian Peninsula. First to act were the Greeks. On 19 August, the British Foreign Minister Sir Edward Grey received notice Premier Venizelos had placed all Greek naval and military resources at the disposal of the Allies. Seizing on this, the Russians approached the pro-German Greek King Constantine; would he consider providing an expeditionary force to assist an attack on the Dardanelles? Both sets of eyes were focused on Constantinople.

A combination of circumstances led to the evolution of the Dardanelles expedition – which would gradually spiral out of control – and which would consume all its originators and have lasting effects on their lives. The entry of the Ottoman Empire into the conflict left the Allies with little choice but to demonstrate their intention that this would not be taken lightly. The Russians in particular sought to show, by arms, that the Ottoman decision to side with the Central Powers was unwise.

Dawning in the minds of the British, was the old concept, exercised since the late nineteenth century, of the 'Forcing of the Dardanelles' in order to threaten Constantinople – especially if the north shore of the Straits, the Gallipoli Peninsula, could be taken in force by the Greeks, and if the Russians could be on hand to meet the Allies at Constantinople. This would surely lead to the surrender of the Ottomans, thereby removing the threat to Egypt and the Suez Canal. In November 1914, at the first meeting of the War Council set up to advise the Cabinet on directions in the war, Sir Winston Churchill, First Lord of the Admiralty, reignited the Dardanelles question by suggesting the best way to protect Egypt and the Suez Canal was to 'capture' the Gallipoli Peninsula; he was to persuade the council that this would be possible by purely naval action on 13 January 1915. The scene was set for the Gallipoli landings.

On 3 January 1915, the Admiralty signalled to Admiral Carden, commanding the Eastern Mediterranean Squadron, for his views on the forcing of the Dardanelles. As First Sea Lord, Churchill had hopes that the age-old naval concept of pitting ships' guns against stone fortresses in 'Forcing' a passage through the Dardanelles Straits could be achieved. However, knowing that the Dardanelles were well-defended, Carden was cagey with his political masters, replying: 'I do not consider Dardanelles can be rushed. They might be forced by extended operations with large numbers of ships.' This cautious, politically worded statement was taken as positive by the Admiralty, who asked Carden to expand his ideas. His detailed four-stage plan that followed involved the reduction of the forts at Sedd el Bahir and Kum Kale at the mouth to the Dardanelles, destroying the inside defences up to Kephez at the entrance to the Narrows, then reducing the forts at the Narrows and, finally, clearing the minefield, reducing the defences above the Narrows, and advancing into the Sea of Marmara. The plan was careful and cautious, but it caught the imagination of Winston Churchill, who, almost by seeing the plan written down, could imagine it being executed in theatre. It would be Carden's plan that would ignite the flames; Carden himself would bear the responsibilities heavily.

Yet the feeling at the Admiralty was that a combined operation was to be preferred to a purely naval attempt, and that troops would be needed to follow up a naval success and clinch the matter; the Gallipoli Peninsula and Constantinople would have to be occupied. With the Greeks and Russians involved, there could surely be no doubt about success; but there was no guarantee that their initial diplomatic advances would come to any concrete proposals. The Secretary of State for War, Field Marshal Lord Kitchener's view was that no British troops were available other than those already committed. Kitchener, a high autocrat, was careful in his husbanding of military resources, and resistant to all schemes to widen the war to other fronts, thereby diverting valuable manpower from the only front that engaged the Germans fully – in France and Flanders. In his mind, the Western Front would have to come first, and the war would be long and costly. However, the Admiralty considered that it would not do much harm to carry out a purely naval attempt in the Dardanelles, a demonstration laid on primarily for benefit of the Russians.

ADMIRAL CARDEN

Admiral Sir Sackville Hamilton Carden had served in Egypt and Sudan and with the Atlantic Fleet until appointed Superintendant of the Malta Dockyard in 1912, finally commanding the British squadron of a joint French-British Mediterranean Fleet in September 1914. When asked to report on its feasibility, Carden's careful strategy for forcing the Dardanelles called for slow, line-abreast advance of the fleet, and the systematic destruction of Turkish fortifications. His plan was successful up to a point; but the strain of the command, and the responsibilities of his plan, meant that he would suffer a nervous breakdown; he would be replaced in early March by Admiral John de Robeck, retiring from the Royal Navy in 1917.

3. Artillery forts either side of the Narrows: at Kilid Bahr (above) and Chanak (Çanakkale, below). The fleet fully expected to be able to bombard these into submission, but it would also have to contend with minefields, torpedoes and mobile batteries. The minelayer Nusret, pictured next to the fort at Çanakkale (below, left), was hero of the hour.

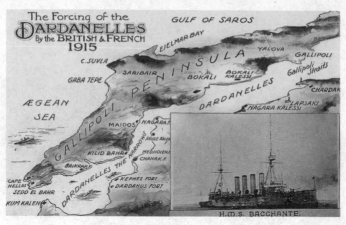

4. Forcing the Dardanelles: a contemporary postcard celebrating the Allied naval failure. Featured is HMS Bacchante, *a British cruiser that would provide naval artillery support for the Anzac landings.*

So, Winston Churchill would declare at the War Council, that: 'The Admiralty should prepare for a naval expedition in February to bombard and take the Gallipoli Peninsula with Constantinople as its objective.' There was a hint of military objectives too; in addition to ships, a naval 'Special Service Force' of two battalions of Royal Marine Light Infantry was prepared for Dardanelles service and sent out to the Island of Lemnos on 6 February 1915 'to be used as demolition parties against forts and batteries'. The scene was set for greater military engagement – and ultimately the landings at Gallipoli. Mudros would be the scene of gathering momentum in the coming weeks.

> The scene in Mudros harbour on April 24th was indeed splendid and inspiring. The natural harbour is immense, and it was crowded with the huge armada assembled there. The whole of de Robeck's fleet and the vast number of transports, supply ships and small craft, provided a spectacle.
>
> General Sir Ian Hamilton

THE ARMIES

The Allied Forces at Gallipoli were truly multinational, with troops from the British and French Empires all serving, facing an Ottoman Army that consisted of both Turk and Arab divisions. In fact there was to be an even greater mix – the Greeks had long planned an attack on the Dardanelles and Kitchener's plan considered, long term, the meeting of the Allies in Constantinople, with Russian forces pressing from the east. With the Greek promise of troops evaporating quickly, the hopes of the Allies of pressing on past the Bulair Lines, tracking along the shores of the Sea of Marmara on to Constantinople, and of Russian assistance, faded fast.

The Ottoman Defenders

The Ottoman Empire had existed since the thirteenth century, but was contracting fast; the Balkan Wars of 1912–13 fought against Serbia, Bulgaria and Greece had seen to that. With several nations vying for control of the Dardanelles and ultimately of Constantinople, the Thracian possessions of the empire had been eroded such that there was only a small tract of land that could be counted as Europe, the remainder being that of Anatolia and farther south into Arabia and Palestine. Committed to the Central

Powers from 1 August 1914 (part of the Kaiser's dream of a Berlin to Baghdad railway), the Ottoman Empire was to be pressed on three fronts: in the Caucasus against the Russians, in the Middle East from Palestine to Mesopotamia against the British and Empire troops and Arab Militias, and in the Dardanelles against the French and British.

Having received setbacks against modern European armies, the Ottoman Empire had pinned its hopes on modernising its army along the lines of the German Empire, victors in the Franco-Prussian war of 1870–71, and the most powerful in Europe. It did so through the use of so-called 'Military Missions', initially that of von der Goltz in the late nineteenth century (1886–95), and later, Liman von Sanders (1913–18). Serving as advisors on training and strategy, these small missions had an effect that was disproportionate to their size, and ensured that the Ottoman officer class was of a very high standard, particularly after Sultan Abdul Hamid II was overthrown in the Young Turk Revolution of 1909. From this point on, there would be great modernisation of the Ottoman Empire, especially following the crushing defeats of the Balkan Wars, with new modern weapons ordered from Europe, the German training of a new officer class, and the increased powers of conscription, applied to all subjects, whether Christian or Muslim.

The Ottomans' position was originally defensive, holding the Russians in the Caucasus and ensuring that the Dardanelles defences were intact and supported by the laying of minefields. With Allied pressure on both Germany and Austria-Hungary, this defensive position was itself under threat, and the Ottomans were pressed to attack the British in the Suez Canal Zone, as well as the Russians in Sarikamish in a disastrous attack in the dead of winter. Both would be setbacks for the Ottomans, and for their Minister for War, Enver Pasha, one of the three Young Turks in power. Yet von Sanders would fall from favour in opposing the Caucasus affair; he would be recalled when the Ottoman homeland was to be threatened directly by the Allies.

5. *Enver Pasha, one of the Young Turks and Ottoman Minister for War. Although he mistrusted Liman von Sanders for his opposition to the ill-fated Caucasus campaign, ultimately he was to place the German in command of the Fifth Army, defending the Gallipoli Peninsula.*

Enver Pascha, Türkischer Kriegsminister

The Ottoman Forces were mobilised in August 1914 with initially three armies, growing to five in 1915. In 1914, the First and Second Armies were serving in Thrace to the west of Constantinople, facing the enemies of the Balkan Wars, and in 1915, defending both shores of the Dardanelles and Bosphorus (the Second Army later serving in the Caucasus); the Third Army served in north-east Anatolia throughout its existence; the Fourth Army, formed in September 1914, was sent to Syria, and took part in the expedition against the British in the Suez Canal Zone in late 1914; and, the Fifth Army, founded on 25 March 1915, was to form the main defence of the Dardanelles against the Allied attacks. Three other armies, the Sixth, Seventh (both formed in 1915) and Eighth (formed in 1917) would see service in Mesopotamia (Iraq), Palestine and Syria.

The Ottoman forces at Gallipoli were predominantly ethnic Turks, but there would be other nationalities, with at least two regiments, the 72nd and the 77th, that were derived from the Arabian Peninsula. With the Ottoman Empire in an almost perpetual state of war since 1911, its troops were battle-hardened and well-disciplined – a factor that would play in their favour during the landings. In addition to such infantry, there would also be local *Gendarmerie* units, battalions derived from

6. Ottoman troops present arms. Following the defeat of the hard-pressed Ottoman Army in the Balkan Wars, the Allies had developed a low opinion of their fighting capabilities. This was to prove wholly unjustified.

the police force, which was run on military grounds; usually named for their place of origin, the *Gendarmerie* would guard coasts and other sensitive locations, but would serve as infantry when the occasion demanded.

The Ottoman Army had been subject to reorganisation since the Balkan Wars had highlighted its inadequacies. Guided by the German military mission, in part it employed German officers, which threw up some misunderstandings, not only due to the language difficulties, but also in the abrupt manner in which German officers were used to dealing with their men. This did not read across to the Ottoman way. It was usual for divisions to be commanded by colonels (identified by the honour *bey*; junior officers are indicated by *efendi*), with generals (honour title, *pasha*) commanding armies. Liman von Sanders *Pasha* would be the most prominent general in this campaign; Mustafa Kemal *Bey* his most celebrated divisional commander. Even given these differences, where Germans were in command they had an unerring respect for their soldiers; a respect that was repeated in the Allied ranks (though not, at first, with the High Command).

UNDERESTIMATING THE OTTOMANS

General Hamilton and the Allies in general had developed a low opinion of the Ottoman military, which was at odds with the facts. The Ottomans' poor showing in both the expedition against the Suez Canal and in the Battle of Sarikamish (fought in the depth of winter) had cemented a prejudice born from the defeats of the Balkan Wars preceding the Great War. In a telegram to Ian Hamilton on 19 April Lord Kitchener reported that the Ottomans had 'displayed an admirable spirit' in fighting near Basra. They were 'well-disciplined, well-trained, and brave'. Yet his telegram also reported the retirement of the enemy in the night; Hamilton had hopes that this would also occur in Gallipoli.

Of greatest importance in reorganising the Ottoman Army was the needs of artillery; all indications had shown that artillery was to play the greatest part in any modern military campaign, and most stockpiles had been practically exhausted during the Balkan Wars. One of the most important components of the alliance struck with the Germans in August 1914 was munitions, to be supplied by the Germans in quantity, with Enver requesting 500,000 shells and 200,000 modern Mauser rifles, followed by a wide range of other war materiel, from uniforms to howitzers, all necessary if the Ottomans were to operate as a viable ally.

The Ottoman artillery was predominantly mountain and field guns, with few heavy guns – these would be supplied by the German and Austrian munitions works during the war, and others would be removed from the Dardanelles defences to attack the invaders. However, the opportunity to hold the high ground and develop static artillery positions was to play in their favour, and the chance of counterbattery work by the Allies was limited. Of particular irritation to the Allies were guns firing at them from the other side of the Dardanelles Straits; with the navy largely withdrawn there was little that could be done about these, nicknamed both 'Asiatic

7. An Ottoman mountain gun battery in Gallipoli. Though short of guns and ammunition, Ottoman artillery fire was accurate and harrying.

Annie' and 'Beachy Bill'. For transport, like the Allies, the Ottoman Army was dependant to a large extent on draft and pack animals, appropriate in a country with little in the way of metalled roads.

Using time gifted to him by the Allied hesitation in pressing the attacks against the static forts of the Dardanelles, and the decision to land troops on the Peninsula, von Sanders was to organise the Ottoman Fifth Army in preparing trenches, barbed wire defences, static strongpoints and heavy weaponry. His knowledge of military engineering and the experience of the Fifth Army, composed of seasoned troops who had been through the Balkan Wars, was to hold von Sanders in good stead. Thus, he was able to ensure that the Allied military assault on the Peninsula was corralled into three small sectors (Helles, Anzac and Suvla), never to be consolidated. Von Sanders' defensive strategy would hold good.

With the military effectiveness of the Ottoman Empire declining, in 1918 Liman von Sanders took over from Erich von Falkenhayn in command of the Ottoman forces in Palestine, who were being

Liman von Sanders

Lieutenant General Otto Liman von Sanders (1855–1929) was appointed head of the German Military Mission to the Ottoman Empire in 1913, and was to go on to take a key role in Ottoman defence of the Gallipoli Peninsula, and to be the architect of its anti-invasion strategy. The Military Mission formed part of the Ottoman strategy of modernisation of its armed forces, with the most powerful of the military nations – Germany with its army and Great Britain its navy – providing advice (and, of course, hoping to increase their own spheres of influence). Following the bungled appropriation of the two Ottoman ships in British shipyards, ultimately it was the Germans who would hold sway. With von Sanders in charge, and following the secret Turco-German Alliance of 1 August 1914, the direct influence of the mission would grow. Following opening of hostilities, the Ottomans would have a series of dramatic reverses against the Allies: Djemal Pasha's Suez Offensive of January–February 1915 against the British was to fail, losing 1,500 dead (at a loss of twenty-two British), while Enver Pasha's Battle of Sarikamish against the Russians in the Caucasian winter of 1914–15 delivered 60,000 battle casualties. Thoroughly beaten, Enver, the Ottoman Minister for War, returned to the capital to take charge of its military forces, and ultimately would turn over the defence of Istanbul, the Dardanelles and the Bosphorus to Liman von Sanders.

8. General Liman von Sanders, the German Commander of the Fifth Ottoman Army. Von Sanders served with the German Military Mission modernising the Ottoman Army prior to the war; he would play an important role in defending the Gallipoli Peninsula from the Allied invasion.

pursued by the British. Von Sanders' strategy would be defensive here too, by stopping the Ottomans in their retreat in order to dig in and meet their enemy from prepared positions. However, in this case General Edmund Allenby's well-organised and mobile British and Empire forces, supported by the Royal Air Force, would force the rout of the Ottomans at the Battle of Megiddo in September 1918. This battle saw the destruction of the Yildrim Army Group commanded by von Sanders, including the Seventh Army, led by Mustafa Kemal, and would lead ultimately to the loss of 75,000 Ottomans, killed, wounded or captured during the Palestine campaign. Almost captured himself during the battle, von Sanders was arrested in Malta in 1919 on the charge of war crimes, but was to be acquitted and released. He was to die in Germany in 1927, aged seventy-four.

9. 'Gallipoli Star' – an Ottoman gallantry medal instigated in 1915, and which is commonly associated with the campaign. Both von Sanders and Kemal are seen wearing this distinctive badge. This example is the poorer quality Ottoman version; German examples are in silver and enamel.

OTTOMAN GALLIPOLI STAR

The *Harp Madalyasi* ('Gallipoli Star', in German *Eiserner Halbmond*, the Iron Crescent) was an Ottoman decoration that was awarded for 'distinguished war service', ranking just below the *Liyakat* medal. First instigated on 1 March 1915, it is a red-enamelled (or painted), five-pointed star bearing the cipher or *toughra* of Sultan Mehmed Reshad V, together with the date 1333 (i.e. 1915 using the Gregorian calendar). Like the Iron Cross, it was a decoration, not a campaign medal; at Çanakkale (Gallipoli) members of the Ottoman forces were undoubtedly awarded this for their bravery. Both Liman von Sanders *Pasha* and Mustafa Kemal *Bey* wore this decoration.

Mustafa Kemal

Mustafa Kemal (1881–1939) was one of the Young Turks; as staff captain in the Third Army he was to join the secret Committee of Union and Progress and took an active part in the Young Turk Revolution in July 1908. Kemal served in the Ottoman Army from 1911.

Kemal was to be tested on several occasions, and was injured by flying rock fragments after an air raid in January 1912. This eye injury would trouble him all his life. In December 1912, Kemal became Commander of Ottoman forces in Gallipoli during the First Balkan Wars, and saw for himself the strength of the Bulair Lines at the neck of the Peninsula, taking part in an unsuccessful amphibious landing, that was repulsed by Bulgarian forces. This lesson would undoubtedly play in Kemal's mind during the Gallipoli campaign.

Kemal was an inspirational leader and on at least two occasions he led his men from the front in repelling the Allies. Though his role in the campaign has been reassessed by historians, he still emerges as a powerful force in the defence of the heights of Sari Bair in particular, successfully limiting the Allied attacks in both April and August 1915. After Gallipoli Kemal would serve in the Caucasus, commanding the XVI Corps of the Ottoman Second Army, and rose to command the Second Army, and then Seventh Army in Palestine a year later.

The post-war partitioning of the Ottoman Empire, and the occupation of Turkish soil by the Allies sparked off the Turkish War of Independence, and led to the growth in Kemal's influence; ultimately he would lead his country out of difficult times to create the modern, secular nation of Turkey, and be its first President, up to his death in 1939.

10. Colonel Mustafa Kemal in Gallipoli. Kemal, commander of the 19th Division in the Ottoman Fifth Army, would be instrumental in holding the Anzac perimeter; his role would be talismanic for the Ottoman soldiers.

Mehmetçik/Johnny Turk

The profile of the Ottoman soldier had changed through the experience of the Balkan Wars, and had seen a shift in influence away from the French to the Germans, a by-product of the crushing defeat of the Franco-Prussian War of 1870–71. Prior to the Young Turk Revolution, the *Mehmetçik* (the Ottoman nickname for the private soldier; he would be 'Johnny Turk' or simply 'Abdul' to the British and Anzacs) wore a blue uniform with red *tarbush* ('fez'); with the reforms of the army, and in line with most other military forces, the standard uniform, introduced in 1909, was drab in colour ('khaki', but varying considerably in shade, from beige to brown, and quality, particularly as the war progressed), its tunic resembling that of the German Army. Rank was indicated by stars and braid on the shoulder straps, and by braid stripes on the sleeves for NCOs. Puttees and boots were worn with breeches. The *tarbush* was replaced with a unique piece of headgear, the *kabalak*, sometimes called the *Enveriye* after Enver Pasha, who introduced it. The *kabalak* consisted of a long cloth that was wound around a wicker base, forming a kind of solar topee. The soldier was armed with a Mauser pattern rifle, known as the Turkish Mauser, usually from two patterns the M1893 and M1903, with appropriate bayonets, both made in Germany. The soldiers' personal equipment, also supplied by their allies, was based on the standard German pattern of leather belt and ammunition pouches, entrenching tool, water bottle and breadbag. This

equipment set represents the ideal; in reality the Ottoman soldier would have to suffer extreme shortages, and would present a rag-tag image to the usually well-equipped Allies.

11. Fully equipped Ottoman infantryman, wearing distinctive headdress and carrying full marching equipment, with Ottoman Mauser rifle. In practice, Ottoman soldiers would wear a great variety of clothing at the front.

The Mediterranean Expeditionary Force (MEF)

Britain had entered the First World War with just four regular infantry battalions capable of forming an expeditionary force to serve in France. Its international commitments meant that other battalions were serving overseas, protecting the outposts of empire; there were also battalions of the Territorial Army, intended initially as primarily a force for Home Defence (though most men volunteered for overseas service), and later in the war, newly raised volunteer and conscript forces. There would also be regular cavalry regiments – which were to be chronically underused in their intended role during the war, together with the Territorial Force's own cavalry – the Yeomanry. By 1915, most of the regular and a large majority of the Territorial Army battalions were being deployed overseas, second line Territorials taking the place of regular troops in some of the quieter outposts – thereby allowing the regular battalions to return home for war service.

When General Sir Ian Hamilton was given the task of commanding the Mediterranean Expeditionary Force, he was told that it would consist of the 30,000 raw Australian and New Zealand (ANZAC) troops then in training in Egypt, the British 29th Division, and the largely untried Royal Naval Division (RND), who would fight alongside their French allies under, in sequence, Generals d'Amade, Gourard and Bailloud. The 29th Division was assembled in the UK from mostly regular infantry battalions that had returned home from foreign stations. As the last regular infantry division to be formed, its fate was surely to be the Western Front, especially as early 1915 was to be a trying time for the British Expeditionary Force (BEF) in France and Flanders. Given that there had been setbacks for the Russians on the Eastern Front, it was felt that the Germans could afford to send reinforcements from the east to west, thereby increasing the pressure on the Allies. As such, Kitchener was notoriously reluctant to commit his last regulars to a campaign that was at best risky; once the naval

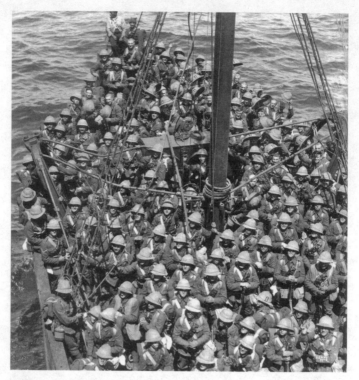

12. Men of the 125th (Lancashire Fusiliers) Brigade arriving at Gallipoli as part of the 42nd (East Lancashire) Division. Thrown straight into the fight, these men would serve through the hard battles for Krithia in May–June 1915.

campaign was agreed and the threat from the east subsided, the 29th was 'loaned' to Hamilton. With men of what was termed the 'Incomparable 29th', it was felt that the task was to be an easier one. The 29th Division was composed of men from the regular battalions of some of Britain's oldest and most respected infantry regiments, its establishment was to be completed with the addition of one Territorial battalion: the 1/5th Royal Scots – which itself would be replaced by the 1st Battalion Newfoundland Regiment. All would receive accolades for their service at Gallipoli, suffering some of the highest casualty figures of the war.

Sir Ian Hamilton

General Sir Ian Hamilton was appointed to the Command of the Constantinople Expeditionary Force – quickly renamed the Mediterranean Expeditionary Force for obvious security reasons. A personal friend of Winston Churchill, Hamilton was one of the country's most experienced generals. He trained at the Royal Military Academy Sandhurst in 1870. Hamilton saw action in the Afghan War, the First Boer War (where he was captured and returned), the Nile Expedition of 1884–85, Burma and in India. He rose through the ranks during this interval, and was decorated. His left arm was badly injured during the Tirah campaign of 1897–98; this arm would remain frail during the rest of his life.

Hamilton also served in the Second Boer War and took active part in several battles, being recommended for the Victoria Cross. He became Kitchener's Chief of Staff. An intelligent soldier, Ian Hamilton was a natural choice as a military observer, and in this capacity took part in the Russo-Japanese War of 1904–05, seeing at first hand the destructive power of modern artillery and machine guns, and the inevitable slide to entrenched warfare. This would influence his thinking in the coming world conflict.

Hamilton's most testing command came in March 1915, when Kitchener appointed him commander-in-chief of the military forces intended to support the naval campaign in the Dardanelles. Kitchener's instructions were brief and to the point. Hamilton was to assemble all military forces available to him so that 'their full weight can be thrown in' to ensure that the navy could force the passage of the Dardanelles.

Hamilton had at his disposal around 70,000 men – to rise as the campaign dragged on. Ultimately, he would fail to meet his objectives, the Gallipoli Peninsula was never taken, the Narrows never reached, the guns never silenced. On 16 October 1915, he was relieved from his command, his once glittering military career in tatters. He was never again to hold meaningful command. He died in 1947.

13. General Sir Ian Hamilton.

Hamilton also had use of the Royal Naval Division, Winston Churchill's 'private army' composed of Royal Naval reservists who were surplus to requirements – there were simply not enough ships for these men to serve in their traditional role. Instead, they were converted to a military role, serving with naval ranks but in the capacity of infantry. The RND had many rising stars in its ranks – men who had joined in order to expedite their move to the frontline. One such was the poet Rupert Brooke, who, tragically, was to die from an infected insect bite while on route to Gallipoli. The RND would also be supplemented by men of the Royal Marine Light Infantry (RMLI).

As the campaign progressed, and progressed, so the commitment of troops continued. The MEF was eventually to have two Army Corps (in addition to ANZAC, discussed below), with ten divisions in total split between the VIII and IX Corps. Variable in experience, the reinforcements would include both Territorial (the 42nd, 52nd, 53rd, 54th and 2nd Mounted), and 'New Army' (the 10th, 11th, 13th) divisions, the latter comprising men who had volunteered for service for the duration of the war, and who had little or no previous military experience. The 2nd Mounted Division

14. A British 60 pounder howitzer taking part in the Third Battle of Krithia. The British artillery would be poorly served by the 'Shell Scandal', which first broke in France in May 1915. Its effects would be hard felt in Gallipoli.

'The Old Sweat'

Landing at the beaches of Gallipoli on 25 April were men who had served in the army for some time, used to iron discipline and therefore steady under fire. This was just as well, as the beaches would become an inferno as the well-disciplined defenders waited for them to disembark before pouring fire into their ranks.

The typical Old Sweat was well-equipped. With no concession to the climate, he wore the standard uniform of the British soldier of the time: a drab (khaki) wool serge uniform that had been first issued in 1902, comprising a jacket that buttoned to the neck, trousers and puttees, it was finished with leather boots and a serge peaked cap (many were to wear a shapeless winter pattern cap known to sergeant majors as the 'Gor'blimey') with regimental cap badge. (Steel helmets, first issued in late 1915, were not to make an appearance at Gallipoli). In battle each man would have an innovative set of cotton webbing equipment, with pouches to hold 150 rounds of .303 ammunition, entrenching tool, water bottle and haversack. He would also carry the Mark III SMLE (Short Magazine Lee Enfield) rifle, which was to be a standard arm of the British soldier into the Second World War. Relatively short compared to the long Mauser carried by the Ottomans, the Old Sweat would carry a long sword bayonet (pattern 1907), in order to ensure he had the same reach as his Mauser-equipped enemy in a bayonet fight.

15. British soldier of the Army Service Corps wearing serge uniform and a Gor'blimey hat. This uniform was worn by the soldiers of the 29th Division in Gallipoli, though as a member of the transport corps, this soldier is not equipped as an infantryman.

'The Terrier'

The Territorial (and New Army) soldiers who were committed to the Dardanelles in the summer of 1915 were kitted out for warmer climes. This would cause issues when summer turned to the blizzard conditions experienced in November on the Peninsula. The standard dress worn by British soldiers in warm climates was Khaki Drill – a uniform of lightweight cotton consisting of jacket and trousers. Worn again with puttees and leather boots, the trousers were often replaced by shorts in hotter conditions. The jacket still buttoned up to the neck, but the uniform could be worn in what was termed 'shirt sleeve order', the jacket discarded to the pack or battalion lines, and soldiers wearing instead the collarless 'grey back' grey-blue woollen shirt. Topping off this uniform was the Wolseley Pattern sun helmet, a large cork helmet designed to keep the sun's rays from beating down on the heads of the soldiers – but gave no more ballistic protection than the normal soft cap. This had a distinctive cloth known as the puggaree wound around it, sometimes with regimental insignia attached. In most cases, the 'Terrier' would wear the same webbing equipment worn by the 'Old Sweat', but at least one territorial battalion landed at Gallipoli with the older 1902 pattern bandolier equipment, comprising leather bandolier and belt pouches with room for 200 rounds of .303 ammunition, and separate water bottle and haversack strung across the body. Some of the New Army battalions would also carry leather equipment – this time the emergency 1914 pattern leather sets. Most would be equipped with the SMLE rifle, like their regular colleagues.

16. *Private Robert Wheatley of the 6th Yorkshire Regiment, pictured in Mudros harbour, 1915. Private Wheatley would be killed in August 1915, in Suvla Bay. He wears Khaki Drill and is equipped with the Wolseley Pattern sun helmet, and a leather bandolier.*

was composed of dismounted Yeomanry – serving in Gallipoli without their horses.

In addition to the infantry were the associated artillery and engineer units. The Royal Regiment of Artillery was composed of three components, Royal Horse Artillery (RHA) and Royal Field Artillery (RFA) manned field guns (13 and 18 pounders: flat trajectory, rapid firing guns), while men of the Royal Garrison Artillery (RGA) were equipped with howitzers and other heavy guns. The terrain at Gallipoli was to cause problems, as was the shortage of shells and guns – in the eyes of the 'Western' generals, opposed to the so-called 'sideshows', it was bad enough that manpower would be diverted away from the Western Front, but to divert badly needed materiel as well would be seen as a crime. The Royal Corps of Engineers were also ever present – their Field Companies had the job of field engineering, sapping and mining, road and jetty construction, light railway support, water supply and signalling.

The Australian and New Zealand Army Corps

The Australian and New Zealand Army Corps (ANZAC) was formed in Egypt; en route for Europe during the Northern Hemisphere winter, North Africa seemed a logical choice to complete their training before being transferred to the front. With the developing situation in the Near East, that front was to be Gallipoli, and the Anzacs were amongst the first to be committed to the campaign.

The Australian government had offered Britain an Expeditionary Force of 20,000 men at the outbreak of war, and recruiting was actively pursued throughout Australia in order to provide a new army for the duration of hostilities. New Zealand was also fully committed to the conflict in Europe – both saw the defence of Britain as the defence of the homeland, the mother country. Not surprisingly, it is estimated that at least 40 per cent of the men who served were British by birth; yet the Anzacs would be lionised in the British press almost as a race of supermen, a view that continues

'THE CHANCE OF A LIFETIME'

Recruiting for the Australian Imperial Forces employed a lot of persuasion, and, in many cases, misinformation. One campaign offered a 'Free Tour to Great Britain and Europe', 'The Chance of a Lifetime'. In order 'to participate in this unique offer', potential soldiers had to be between eighteen and forty-five, with a minimum height of 5ft 2in. – the same requirements for the British Army.

to the present day. Certainly, the Australian official historian, Charles E.W. Bean held that opinion (while being critical of some of the British troops of the campaign). The Anzacs would be rightly celebrated for their bravery – and ambivalence to military discipline.

Troopships from the main cities in Australia and New Zealand had assembled at King George Sound in Western Australia, and went to Egypt in two convoys. The first to leave was on 7 November 1914, the next on 31 December. The journey was not without drama; HMAS *Sydney*, a light cruiser protecting the troop convoy, was directed to leave and attack the German raider SMS *Emden*, fatally damaging her in the Battle of the Cocos, on 9 November. The stricken ship would be seen – and photographed – by all subsequent Anzac troopships that passed by.

In Egypt, the men of the Australian and New Zealand Army Corps were to be camped close to Cairo, the Australians adjacent to the pyramids of Giza – ancient monuments that would figure heavily in posed photos sent home. Training was hard but in some ways a little unreal amongst the ancient monuments of Egypt, and famously, on Good Friday 1915, the Anzacs fought the 'Battle of the Wazzir', a riot in the Red Light district of Cairo.

The Australian and New Zealand Army Corps was composed of the 1st Australian Division, the composite New Zealand and Australian Division, comprising the New Zealand Infantry

17. Men of the Australian and New Zealand Army Corps training at Giza, Egypt, with the pyramids behind. Many more pictures, with soldiers seated on camels, would be staged for the people back home.

18. Australian field battery in action in Gallipoli. The difficulty of the terrain at Anzac meant that the deployment of field guns such as these was a difficult proposition. High trajectory howitzers were sorely needed.

Brigade, the 4th Australian Infantry Brigade, and the 1st Light Horse Brigade and New Zealand Mounted Rifles Brigade, both originally mounted; General W.R. Birdwood was selected to command the force. In addition to the infantry and Light Horse/ Mounted Rifles components there were also Australian artillery, engineer and medical services – with the additional 7th Indian Mountain artillery. Most of the artillery would be equipped with the standard 18 pounder field guns used by the British Army, with a smaller component of heavier howitzers. In all cases, the artillery support available to the MEF was inadequate.

19. The Gallipoli Star. This campaign medal was planned but never issued; it was intended for all members of the Australian and New Zealand Army Corps, but was not awarded; the British 1914–15 star had to suffice for all.

ANZAC GALLIPOLI STAR

A special campaign medal was originally to be awarded to all Anzac participants of the Gallipoli campaign. It was to be in the form of the star, bearing a central crown and the legend 'Gallipoli 1914–15' (referring to all who had participated in the Gallipoli campaign, and who had sailed in 1914). Its ribbon was to have two outer edges of yellow and silver, symbolic of the wattle (Australia) and fern (New Zealand) respectively, and a central band of blue separated from the yellow and silver by two narrow red stripes (symbolising the army). It was never awarded – the King did not sanction a medal that was to be given to the Anzacs alone, when so many other men served. The British 1914–15 campaign medal served for all.

William Birdwood

William Birdwood (1865–1951) was born in India and trained at the Royal Military College in Sandhurst before joining first the Royal Scots Fusiliers, and then the Indian Army, in which he served as a cavalry officer. In the late nineteenth century he saw action on the North-West Frontier with both the 12th Lancers and the Bengal Lancers. During the Second Boer War (1899–1902) he served on Lord Kitchener's staff, together with Ian Hamilton. After the war he returned to the North-West Frontier, and was later promoted to major general in 1911.

Birdwood's association with Australia came through Lord Kitchener's instruction of November 1914 that he should form an army corps from the Australian and New Zealand troops that were training in Egypt before moving to France and Flanders – here was born the Australian and New Zealand Army Corps (ANZAC). Later to be transferred to the Dardanelles, forming part of the Allied units landing in April 1915, with General Birdwood in command. He had been led by Kitchener to believe that he would be in charge of the whole operation, but this was not the case. However, promoted to lieutenant general in October 1915, he took command of all British and Empire army corps in the Dardanelles Army, under Ian Hamilton, with the A & NZ Army Corps itself led by General Alexander Godley.

After Gallipoli, Birdwood served as commander of the newly reorganised II Anzac Corps, and took command of the Australian Imperial Force (AIF) as a whole. Promoted to full general in October 1917, he nevertheless remained a corps commander in charge of the five Australian Corps serving on the Western Front. Ultimately he would take command of the Fifth Army in May 1918. After the war,

 he returned to India, becoming a field marshal in 1925, and commanding the British Indian Army until 1930. As a Briton, Birdwood failed in his attempt to become governor general of Australia. Actively involved in the defence of Britain during the Second World War, he died in 1951.

20. General William Birdwood. Birdwood – known as 'Birdie' to Hamilton – was passed over for command of the Mediterranean Expeditionary Force in favour of his old friend in March 1915.

'The Digger'

The 'Digger' was lauded by all observers at the time for his bravery and 'fine physique', and would come to epitomise the spirit of the soldier in adversity. Though the name 'Digger' is associated with the Australian soldier, at the time it applied to all members of the A & NZ Army Corps. As the campaign wore on, Anzacs were more likely to be wearing the remnants of uniform that came to be called 'Gallipoli undress' (cut-down trousers, sleeveless shirts, battered hats), rather than the uniforms they were issued with. The Australian jacket was unusual, made from wool it had distinctive pleats, an integral belt that echoed the then popular Norfolk jacket – and bearing the unique 'rising sun' collar badges and bronze 'Australia' shoulder titles. Worn with breeches, puttees and boots, the whole would be topped off with a peaked cap, or, in many cases, the distinctive slouch hat (which was universally adopted in 1916). New Zealanders wore broadly the same uniform as the British Tommy, however, though distinguished by their own 'lemon-squeezer' hat. While Kiwis also carried British-made 1908 webbing equipment, Australians had their own. Based largely on the British pattern, it was nevertheless made from kangaroo leather – which had a tendency to stretch. Ultimately, the Australians would also adopt cotton webbing. All would carry the SMLE rifle, like their British comrades, but Australian-made.

21. The epitome of Anzac spirit; an Australian sergeant pictured in 1918. He wears the distinctive Australian uniform jacket, and slouch hat. In the heat of the summer, less clothing was the norm: 'Gallipoli undress'.

The 'Rising Sun' badge

Does the 'rising sun' badge of the Australian Imperial Forces actually depict the sun, or does it have more martial origins? While most people accept the idea of the sun insignia, others suggest that it is a design devised by Major General Sir Edward Hutton, the commander of the Australian Military Forces in the Boer War. Hutton had in his possession an arc of swords and bayonets that symbolised the military – and which was deemed to be the best depiction of the new force. Adopted in 1903, it was worn in Gallipoli and every Australian campaign since.

Corps Expeditionaire d'Orient

The Corps Expeditionaire d'Orient was composed of approximately 50 per cent of troops from metropolitan France; the other 50 per cent would be composed of troops from France's colonial possessions.

The Metropolitan Brigade was comprised of a standard 'Territorial' infantry regiment (the 175th), for the most part distinguished by their uniform of *bleu horizon* and kepi (the distinctive French headgear), and a Régiment de marche d'Afrique, formed from two battalions of *zouaves* and a battalion of the Légion Etranger. The *zouaves* were European French soldiers, distinguished, in the early stages of the war at least, by their flamboyant uniform of red trousers and blue short jacket. In Gallipoli, the French were to cut a colourful crowd amongst their Allies. The *zouaves* held a reputation as formidable soldiers, as did their Légion Etranger colleagues, composed of foreign volunteers.

The New Zealanders marvelled to see French officers in blue and red... As a relief from our inevitable khaki, the French Senegalese with their dark blue uniforms, the Zouaves with

22. French colonial troops, consisting of European and Senegalese soldiers, preparing to embark. The role of the French in the Gallipoli campaign has been largely overshadowed by their British and Anzac allies.

their baggy trousers, and the French Territorials with their light blue, imparted quite a dash of colour to the scene.

Major Fred Waite, New Zealand Engineers

The Colonial Brigade was formed of two *régiments mixtes coloniaux*, so-called colonial troops comprised of French citizens and native regiments that were intended to garrison the French colonies. The two regiments serving in the Dardanelles each consisted of two battalions of French Senegalese troops with the addition of a battalion of European French troops, usually raised from reservists or new conscripts. Ian Hamilton would be suspicious of the fighting qualities of the Senegalese; this view would not be shared by his men, particularly those of the Royal Naval Division who served alongside the Africans on Krithia Spur.

The French troops in the Dardanelles would be better served by their artillery than their allies; not only were they equipped with the famous 75mm field gun (or 65mm mountain guns), but they would not suffer the shell shortage that would blight all British offensives in 1915. The '*Soixante-Quinze*' had a unique hydropneumatic recoil action that meant the gun did not have to be re-aimed after each shot, and was capable of firing 15–20 shells a minute – delivering high explosives and shrapnel. Its effects would be felt in the repeated French attempts at carrying the trenches on the right of the British line at Cape Helles.

23. Médaille Commémorative d'Orient, *issued to all members of the French Army that served in the Dardanelles; scant reward for their resilience under fire.*

MÉDAILLE COMMÉMORATIVE D'ORIENT

This medal was not awarded until June 1926. Though it had been mooted during the war, French veterans of the Gallipoli campaign would have to wait ten years for some form of recognition.

Henri Gourard

The French had committed to the Dardanelles on 24 February, with a naval and military presence, the Corps Expeditionaire d'Orient, to serve under the overall command of General Sir Ian Hamilton – who was a fluent French speaker. The French corps were destined to be led by three generals during their time in the campaign: Albert d'Amade (1856–1941) (from its inception until 14 May), Henri Gourard (1867–1946) (from 13 May–3 July), and Bailloud. Of these, it was Gourard that was to have the most pugnacious spirit, with d'Amade roundly criticised for his lack of progress and initiative and Bailloud similarly portrayed as a defensive general.

Henri Gourard was born in Paris, and trained as a soldier at the Saint Cyr Military Academy in 1888, his decision to enter the army motivated by the catastrophic defeat of what was once the greatest military in the world during the Franco-Prussian War of 1870–71. Graduating in 1890, from 1894 he was to achieve fame in France's African colonies of Sudan, Niger, Chad and Mauritania. In the run up to the First World War Gourard, now promoted to *général de brigade*, was ultimately to command all French troops in western Morocco.

Gourard was a young general (at forty-two), and was well liked by Hamilton. With Hunter-Weston he was architect of the French contribution to the successive assaults on Krithia (though also suggesting to Hamilton that another assault could be made at Gaba Tepe). Gourard himself would be injured by a shell, launched by 'Asiatic Annie' in early July, and would be replaced by General Bailloud.

Despite losing an arm, Gourard would eventually return to command the Fourth Army on the Western Front in July 1917, being instrumental in soaking up the pressure from German troops during the Second Battle of the Marne in 1918. After the war, his military

reputation intact, Gourard would serve as representative of the French Government in the Middle East, and in 1920 a controversial High Commissioner for Syria and Lebanon. In 1923, he returned as military governor of Paris, a role he held until 1937. He died in the city of his birth in 1946.

24. General Gourard, commander of the French Corps Expeditionaire d'Orient.

'Le Poilu'

Le Poilu ('hairy-one') was the nickname for all French troops – but in the Dardanelles, the mix of the French forces was very diverse indeed. This also meant that the uniform styles varied considerably.

The standard blue horizon uniform was introduced in 1915 to replace the distinctive style of blue jacket and red trousers – hopelessly unsuited to modern warfare. The uniform comprised a tunic (*vareuse*), trousers, greatcoat (*capotte*), puttees and boots and a kepi (though this was replaced with a *bonnet de police* side cap in France). White pith helmets were also worn by European troops serving with the colonial regiments in Gallipoli, criticised for being too conspicuous.

Rank was indicated on the *vareuse* by chevrons and stripes on the sleeve (for NCOs), and bars for officers (stars for generals). All *poilu* carried the 1893 Lebel rifle (which did not use a charger or clip like the British SMLE or Ottoman Mauser, but required individual loading of its magazine). The equipment carried by the soldier was made of leather, with ammunition pouches, belt, straps and pack – with a great variety of individual items carried in the field.

25. French infantryman carries a wounded comrade in Gallipoli. A poilu *of one of the Metropolitan Brigades in the Dardanelles, he wears a blue horizon uniform and kepi. It was usual for French soldiers to wear their coat (the* capotte*) as an outer battle garment, wearing the tunic (*vareuse*) underneath in colder weather.*

THE DAYS
BEFORE BATTLE

On 16 February 1915, the British War Council (including the Prime Minister Asquith, the First Lord of the Admiralty Sir Winston Churchill, the First Sea Lord 'Jacky' Fisher and the Secretary of State for War Lord Kitchener) made two momentous decisions: the Dardanelles should not only be forced by naval action, but troops should be committed to the operation. Overcoming his original doubts, Kitchener agreed that the British 29th Division, together with the Australian and New Zealand Army Corps, would be sent to the theatre, meeting at the advanced base of the Greek island of Lemnos, notable for its natural harbour of Mudros – but also notable for its almost complete lack of suitable accommodation.

Rear-Admiral Rosslyn Wemyss was dispatched to Lemnos as its new 'Governor', with instructions to oversee the facilities and accommodation. The first troops to arrive were the men of the Royal Naval Division; they found the facilities so inadequate that the base was temporarily moved to Alexandria in Egypt.

With this backdrop of preparation, the naval attack under Carden on the outer forts of the Dardanelles began on 19 February; a strong Anglo-French task force bombarded the static and ancient Ottoman forts at the entrance to the Straits. The attack was to have many successes, and the outer forts were soon

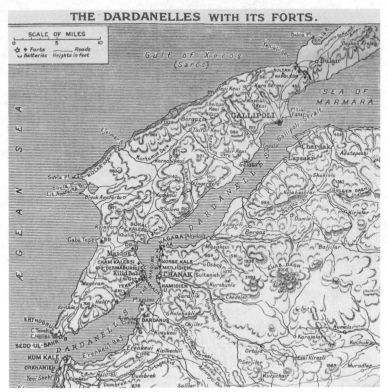

26. Map of the Gallipoli Peninsula, showing the main fortresses and coastal defences that were to be attacked by the Allied fleet. What is not shown are the minefields and other more transient defences.

neutralised – leading both Carden to believe that the passage would be easier than it subsequently proved, and a sense of panic among the defenders who saw both guns and ammunition under attack. Despite this, the responsibilities played heavily on an ailing Carden – original author by default of the naval scheme – who asked to be relieved of his command due to the executive strain. In his place stood Vice-Admiral de Robeck, who would take the responsibility for what would be the last concerted effort – the main attack of 18 March.

27. The fleet steams into the Dardanelles; they would retreat on 18 March, and would gradually be withdrawn from sight by Admiral de Robeck.

On what would come to be celebrated as the Turkish national day, the main attack pitted eighteen ships of the combined British and French fleet in three lines against the narrowest part of the Dardanelles. Here ancient stone-built forts glowered at each other across the Straits. Supporting them were mobile howitzer batteries, difficult to locate; and an even greater danger, minefields. Concerted efforts had been made to try and sweep the channel clear. Sir Roger Keyes, a man of action, had personally led the assorted craft in sweeping the Straits, but had not banked on the *Nusret* (now preserved at the naval museum in Çanakkale), which worked through the night to lay fresh mines. This would prove fatal to the Allied effort.

The guns in the forts were largely silenced by 2pm: 'All telephone wires were cut, all communications with the forts were interrupted, some of the guns had been knocked out... in consequence the artillery fire of the defence had slackened considerably.' And then, disaster befell the Allied lines. The French battleship *Bouvet* struck a mine and was lost with all hands, while HMS *Irresistible* and HMS *Inflexible* were damaged, left vulnerable to further Ottoman attack, as were the French ships *Suffren* and *Gallois*. *Irresistible* would sink – and so would HMS *Ocean*, sent to render assistance to the stricken ship:

> It all happened so suddenly. One minute the *Bouvet* was steaming majestically along, the next moment a tremendous cloud of smoke or steam arose, completely hiding her from view, and after two or three minutes, the smoke clears away, where there had been a gallant ship there now remained a few struggling forms in the water.
>
> Lance Corporal Paver, RMLI, HMS *Irresistible*

In planning the forcing of the Dardanelles, the War Council had glibly talked of using old, obsolete, or outdated ships. What they had not banked on was the loss of the crews of these ships – and now in charge Admiral de Robeck felt the pressure of such losses. He ordered the cessation of the attack – yet all authorities would later write that the Ottoman defences were at the point of collapse (making his decision the first of many 'what-ifs' that mark the campaign). Beaten by minefields and the minefields guarded by the guns, the fleet would back off. It would never return, and its ships would gradually be withdrawn in the coming months due to the threat of ever more aggressive torpedo boat attacks. It was telling that when the troops were landing, the ships they were sent to support would progressively abandon them to their fate – and the whole point of the expedition in the first place would evaporate.

If they had not guessed it before, the Ottoman command definitely knew that a storm was directed at them, and at the Dardanelles in particular. The British were now fully committed: there could be no withdrawal if the navy was to fail in its attempt. The War Council agreed that now it had commenced, the operation must be carried out at all cost. Kitchener expected that the incremental success of Carden's plan would see the Dardanelles

28. HMS Irresistible. *One of the Allied ships that was to suffer at the hands of the Ottoman defences; listing heavily after striking a mine at 4.16pm on 18 March 1915, she would later sink in the deep waters of the Dardanelles.*

forts silenced by degree, the Ottoman Army withdrawing gradually; landings of British troops would guarantee their silence. This was essentially the War Office view that prevailed up to the failure of the great naval attack on the Narrows on 18 March, following which the logic was suddenly reversed – the army must now clear the way for the navy.

On 20 February, Kitchener cabled Lieutenant General Sir John Maxwell, Commander-in-Chief in Egypt, informing him that the fleet had begun an attack on the Dardanelles, and warning him to prepare a force of two divisions (30,000 troops) of the Anzac Corps under General William Birdwood, to be ready to sail from Egypt on about 9 March. In advance of this, Kitchener also ordered Birdwood to make an immediate reconnaissance of the Dardanelles and provide a joint appreciation of the task ahead with Admiral Carden:

Proceed to meet Admiral Carden at the earliest possible opportunity and consult him as to the nature of the combined operations which the forcing of the Dardanelles is to involve. Report the result to me. You should learn, from local observation and information the numbers of the Turkish garrison on the peninsula, and whether the Admiral thinks it will be necessary to take the forts in reverse; if so what force will be required, and generally in what manner it is proposed to use the troops. Will the Bulair lines have to be held, and will operations on the Asiatic side be necessary or advisable.

Field Marshal Lord Kitchener, Secretary of State for War

Apart from making his reconnaissance and appreciation on the Dardanelles combined operation, Birdwood was also asked to inform Kitchener at the same time how he thought additional troops should be employed 'for a further enterprise after the Straits have been forced', a clear reference to the expected advance eastwards towards Constantinople. Birdwood's reconnaissance of the Straits led him to conclude that the immediate landing of troops was needed; the ability of the hidden Ottoman batteries to put down a barrage on the fleet was the real problem, as was their prevention of the all important act of minesweeping. These guns were in 'dead ground', leaving the guns of the fleet unable to locate them.

Based on his appreciation, Birdwood planned to land a strong force at Cape Helles at the toe of the Peninsula, covered by a feint at Bulair, the point where the Peninsula narrows. The Helles force, having secured a bridgehead, would then fight forward to the line Gaba Tepe–Kilid Bahr. This was the line of heights just short of the Narrows, from which position the main forts on the European side of the Dardanelles could be taken in reverse and the hidden batteries on both shores dealt with. Kitchener instructed Birdwood to practise his troops in opposed beach landings. Yet Birdwood's task was still 'To assist the navy... to give any co-operation that

ACHI BABA

The importance of Achi Baba as an artillery observation post was emphasised by many involved in planning the initial operations. Surgeon Rear-Admiral Jeans later repeated the discussions he had heard on board *Euryalus*, between Hamilton and de Robeck about capturing Achi Baba: 'Its summit commanded the whole system of gun positions on both sides of the Dardanelles at Kilid Bahr and Chanak, and once the 15 inch howitzer already at Mudros with its tractor and railway lines, could be mounted there and brought to bear on that system its destruction was anticipated in a few days.'

may be required, and to occupy any captured forts.' Clearly no serious opposition from the Turkish garrison of Gallipoli and the Dardanelles was expected.

The destruction of the defending coast batteries would enable the fleet to push through the Straits and the Bulair Lines to be captured. Undoubtedly there was considerable naval and army agreement on the importance of Achi Baba for such a purpose, but it was based on a misconception; the summit did not in fact give a direct view of the Narrows' defences, which were hidden by intervening high ground and the steep scarp edge of the Kilid Bahr Plateau.

Birdwood had been led to understand by Kitchener that he would be given command of the expanded 'Constantinople Expeditionary Force'. Ultimately, he was to be disappointed; the addition of the Royal Naval Division, the 29th Division and General d'Amade's Corps Expeditionaire d'Orient forced Kitchener to appoint Sir Ian Hamilton, a general of greater rank and experience to the command.

Ottoman Preparations

Having experienced their first shock at the Allied bombardment of the outer defences, the Ottomans prepared for the onslaught on the Straits. With the Allied Fleet fully engaged, it was only a matter of time before the military would press for landings in order to silence the guns, and to allow the minesweepers to do their job. The future of the Ottoman capital was in the hands of the defenders of the Peninsula.

Strategically, the Peninsula was of the greatest importance. A cluster of small plateaux and dissected ridges at its heart, to the south-east the slopes are gentle but deceptive – particularly as centuries of river drainage had cut great grooves down to the sea, and created narrow beaches slotted through steep limestone cliffs. Yet the fact that high ground dominated almost all the beaches available for landing was not lost on the Ottoman commanders. Threatened for centuries, the oldest defences were at its weakest point, adjacent to the Gulf of Saros, a low, narrow neck that had been entrenched and fortified during the Crimean War by the British, when they were housed there, and allied to the Ottomans. The 'Bulair Lines' were a shadow of their former self, but had been used in the Balkan Wars – against Mustafa Kemal himself – and could be used again. Liman von Sanders, commander of the Fifth Army detailed to defend the Peninsula, was alive to the possibilities and deployed three infantry divisions (4th, 5th and 7th) to protect it, and stayed alert, defending them throughout the campaign. Losing the Bulair Lines would mean the Peninsula would be cut off from Constantinople, separating the Ottomans from their main supply lines. However, the 'Lines' were a long way from the Narrows, and the Allied ships were stuck there.

Von Sanders may have been concerned about the 'Lines', but he also knew that the enemy would want to take the Ottoman forts on the Straits from the rear. And this would also mean the possibility of a landing on the Asiatic shore – yet here the enemy would have to face up to the problem that the whole of Anatolia would be there to provide supply and reinforcement, offering a large hinterland to operate within. Other than the possibility of landings at Besika Bay on the Asiatic shore, his real expectations would be that the Allies would land at Cape Helles. Here there were beaches, albeit narrow;

there would be the possibility of a direct naval approach; and, there was the slope leading up to Achi Baba, which would provide the first tantalising glimpses of the Narrows below.

With the collapse of the naval engagement, there was no choice but to proceed with the landings, planned for 23 April 1915. It was understood by both sides that there were two key strategic objectives of a land-based campaign: the command of the Dardanelles Straits, controlling the passage of both naval and merchant ships; and the removal of the threat of both fixed and mobile coastal batteries on the shore of the Dardanelles. And just as the purpose of the campaign was appreciated from both sides, so they were aware that there were a limited number of locations, determined largely by the disposition of major terrain elements, where a landing could be successfully executed: in the northern part of the Peninsula near Bulair, the narrowest part of the isthmus connecting Gallipoli with the rest of Thrace; either side of the promontory known as Gaba Tepe, in a depression separating the two main massifs of the southern peninsula; at the narrow beaches of Cape Helles, threatening the southern slopes of the Kilid Bahr Plateau; and on the Asiatic

GEOGRAPHY AT GALLIPOLI

In a paper read to the Royal Geographical Society on 26 April 1915, the noted archaeologist and expert on the Near East, D.G. Hogarth, outlined the geography of the war with Turkey. This paper, read a day after the landing had been made undoubtedly in ignorance of the land-based assault, holding the following conclusion: 'All the western end of the Gallipoli Peninsula is of broken hilly character, which combines with lack of water and consequent lack of population and roads to render it an unfavourable area for military operations. No general, if he had the choice, would land a considerable force upon it at any spot below the narrows'.

shore of the Dardanelles, notably at Kum Kale at its entrance, and at Besika Bay. A fifth landing site, that of Suvla Bay, was rejected – it was too far away from the Straits, separated from them by high ground. This very fact would haunt General Sir Ian Hamilton in August.

Hamilton also rejected both Bulair and the Asiatic shore as main landing sites. The latter was ruled out because its defensive positions were known to be strong. Bulair would be a bottleneck for troops landing from the Gulf of Saros, vulnerable to the high ground both north-east and south-west. Equally Hamilton abandoned the idea of a massed landing on the Asiatic shore on the grounds that supply would be difficult, and opposition would be strong and easily reinforced, in any case, it was the heights of the Gallipoli Peninsula that commanded the Dardanelles, not the Asiatic shore. Instead, all effort was to be made in the southwestern part of the Peninsula, all expectations fixed on the capture of the Kilid Bahr Plateau which overlooked the Narrows. In so doing this would achieve the primary objective of the landing, the support of naval operations. The main

29. Destroyed gun at Fort No. I (Etrugrul) at the entrance to the Dardanelles – and overlooking the landing beach at Sedd el Bahir. This was wrecked by the Allied bombardment.

landings were therefore to be made at the southern end of the Peninsula at Cape Helles, with diversionary attacks by the Anzacs north of Gaba Tepe, and the French on the Asiatic shore.

Meanwhile, General von Sanders was focused on the potential for landings at Bulair or Besika Bay – the former because of its strategic position in controlling the neck of the Peninsula, the latter because of the possibilities provided by its relatively wide beaches – he knew he would also have to fortify other vulnerable positions, particularly at Cape Helles and Gaba Tepe. Both would receive his attention. While the ships stood off the toe of the Peninsula, the Ottoman troops toiled at fortifying it. As the British commander would observe from the deck of HMS *Queen Elizabeth*:

> The Peninsula itself is being fortified and many Turks work every night on trenches, redoubts and entanglements. All landing places are now commanded by lines of trenches and are ranged by field guns and howitzers.
>
> General Sir Ian Hamilton, 17 March 1915

THE BATTLEFIELD:
WHAT ACTUALLY HAPPENED?

The Gallipoli Peninsula is a small sliver of land jutting defiantly out into the Aegean Sea. Adjacent to mainland Greece – Thrace – the region has seen conflict for centuries, part of the European legacy of the Ottoman Empire. Geologically, the creation of the Dardanelles, the Sea of Marmara (so-called because of the proximity of reserves of pure white marble) and the Bosphorus – waterways which have seen much intrigue and conflict – were created by the tectonic forces that still today periodically bring earthquakes, and resulting human tragedy to the region. These forces also created the offsets and constrictions that are such a peculiarity of the Dardanelles Straits, forcing ships passing through them to be aware of their navigation.

The landscape of Gallipoli is hauntingly beautiful – a fact not lost on the young men who fought there, and the poets who followed. Fragrant, green, teeming with wildlife and with the blue waters of the Aegean lapping its shores, it is no wonder that today tourists from Istanbul come to bathe in the quiet waters and soak up the grandeur of the landscape. Almost 100 years ago it was somewhat different – the scene of great suffering, tragedy and disease. The same landscape was to directly influence the battles here in 1915, recorded in numerous histories of the Gallipoli

30. Modern satellite view of the Dardanelles and the Gallipoli Peninsula, showing the peculiarities of the Straits, offset by tectonic forces and earthquakes. This makes the Dardanelles difficult to navigate, and easier to defend. The high ground of the Peninsula is shown as a dark colour.

campaign which detail the local inadequacy of water supplies, the steepness of the slopes, the incision of its ravines, the precipitous nature of the cliffs, and the density of vegetation. All conspired to make the Dardanelles a trying place to serve in.

Yet the landscape of the Gallipoli Peninsula is also relatively subdued, the dominant features being a series of ridges and plateaux that provide the high ground so sought after by any invading force. The hard ridges forming the northern coast of the Peninsula contrast with the flat-topped but steep-sloped plateaux that form most upland areas of the Peninsula. One of the most prominent uplands of the Peninsula is the Sari Bair Range – the highest hills in the fighting zone of 1915, and a plateau with a steep north-facing cliff, created by the movement of geological faults, throwing up the cliff and creating a natural barrier. Heavily weathered by winter rainfall on soft soils, the slopes are formed

31. 'The Sphinx', hard bands of pebbly rock (conglomerates) have left this distinctive feature of the Anzac battlefield standing proud while the rest of the landscape is weathered back.

of a complex network of sharp-crested ridges, packed with unforgiving scrub, the military term for which would be 'broken ground' – in this case not an exaggeration.

Here and there, harder rock bands create more resistant features, such as 'The Sphinx', a feature named for its resemblance to the Egyptian monument, adjacent to which the Anzac soldiers had camped and exercised. As was apparent to the men on the ground, the Sari Bair Range is dissected by three major gullies that run down to the sea, part of a drainage pattern in which water defines its own parallel path from the peaks to the sea. This creates the amphitheatric form of the Anzac battlefield, in which major gullies became the supply ways, the intervening ridges, three of them, being important strongholds and observation platforms.

In the southeastern part of the Peninsula, the Kilid Bahr Massif forms a counterpart to the Sari Bair Range, divided from it by a belt of low ground, exploited by rivers and man, which passes from Gaba Tepe across the Peninsula to the shore of the Dardanelles, just north of Maidos (now Eceabat), which shelters under the steep cliffs of the Kilid Bahr Plateau. The boundaries of this mountain are more subdued than that of the Sari Bair Range; nevertheless, its northern boundary, a steep slope, glowers down on the low ground that crosses the Peninsula from Gaba Tepe, and which is sharply incised by two valleys running down to the Dardanelles. The second of these, Saghani Dere, is strategically significant, as the broad tract that separates Kilid Bahr from Achi Baba. Both pieces of high ground would be highly sought after objectives, with the strongly fortified Kilid Bahr fortress commanding the Narrows, completely protected by the steep cliffs of the massif that bears its name, and the similar forts at Chanak (now Çanakkale).

Achi Baba (actually Alci Tepe) is also a plateau, its flat top is surmounted by the small, almost rectangular peak of Achi Baba itself, almost a classic 'kopje' – a feature that must have chimed in the memories of Hamilton and other veterans of the South African veldt. The slopes are incised by ephemeral streams that flow north-east and south-west. These streams, particularly those heading for the tip of the Peninsula are strongly gullied, in some cases forming deep ravines – Zighin Dere (Gully Ravine), Kanli Dere and Kereves Dere, all of which serve to break up the Peninsula into the separate broad 'spurs'. This large area of the southern peninsula gives the impression of a long, low-angled glacis, a surface that could in theory be swept by low-trajectory naval gunfire – essential for a lightly armed invading force, and a tantalising vision for the military planners of 1915.

The land-based Gallipoli campaign can be conveniently divided into five main phases: the landings on 25 April (the Battles of the Beaches); the Ottoman counterattacks in the Anzac sector during April; the struggles for the control of Krithia and Achi Baba in May–June; the August offensives; and, the Suvla Bay landings. The sixth phase, that of the withdrawal from the Peninsula in

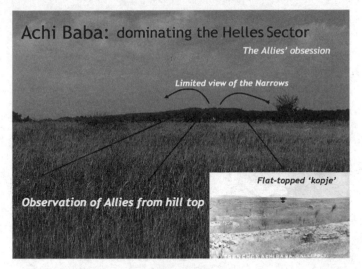

32. *Achi Baba. The focus of Ian Hamilton's attention – and obsession – during the Gallipoli campaign. Heavily entrenched by the Ottomans, the Allies never reached it, despite three broad-front offensives to do so. As the British would find after the war – it would give only limited views of the Narrows.*

December–January, was the inevitable result of the failure of the Allies to make headway.

General Sir Ian Hamilton decided that there were to be three main landing areas, and two feints, all to be attacked on 23 April, although this was delayed by weather conditions to 25 April. The feints at Bulair and Besika Bay were intended to draw Turkish troops away from the main landing areas, and to keep open an element of surprise as to where the main landings were going to take place. The three main landings were at the southern end of the Peninsula, at Cape Helles and Gaba Tepe, and on the Asiatic shore at Kum Kale. The Cape Helles landings were made by the men of the British 29th Division at five beaches, code lettered S, V, W, X and Y. Landings north of Gaba Tepe at Z Beach were to be made by the men of the Australian and New Zealand Army Corps. They were to be landed from towed open boats commanded by

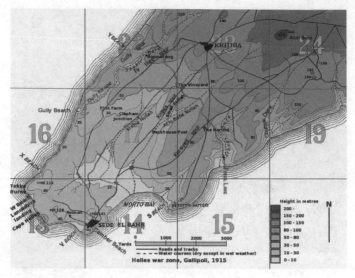

33. The Helles Front, showing the main landing beaches (S, V, W, X, Y), and the location of Achi Baba. Here the Peninsula is divided into four 'spurs' by four river valleys that run parallel to its coasts. These would have a major impact on the outcome of the campaign.

junior naval officers who had orders to stay in set positions as they approached the shore. Finally, the French landing at Kum Kale met with limited opposition, gaining an important bridgehead, which was nevertheless later to be relinquished.

The Battle of the Beaches 25–26 April 1915

In common with all the military commanders, Liman von Sanders knew of the threats to the Dardanelles defences if the beaches were left undefended. He also knew that if the Allies could sterilise the Peninsula by cutting it off at the neck – the Bulair Lines – then the Ottoman defenders would be isolated from assistance, even from the Asiatic shore, and behind it the main mass of the Anatolian Peninsula. For the German commander of the Fifth Ottoman Army, it was essential that his main force be held in reserve, ready to rush to wherever the enemy would appear – and in his view, that threat was either at Bulair – or farther south, at the tip of the Gallipoli Peninsula. However for General Sir Ian Hamilton, there was to be no luxury of time to think. The fleet had stood off, and time was counting down. With each day wasted, so there was opportunity for the enemy to reinforce and reinstate the defences at the Narrows, and to relay minefields that would further decimate the Allied Fleet.

Hamilton's choices had been made. He would land his most experienced division, the 29th, at Cape Helles, divided between all available beaches. In fact, he had little choice but to split up the attacking force – the majority of the beaches just could not contain the great mass of men needed. They would have to be separated – but the idea that all available beaches would be used, some pretty formidable, backed with steep cliffs, was to be a surprise. The fleet would provide the artillery support for the landings, their long range, low trajectory guns intended for naval engagements capable of firing from three sides of the Peninsula, and up the low slope to the prize – Achi Baba.

If the landings were to be a success, then the enemy would need to be occupied. In order to keep von Sanders guessing, Hamilton would deploy the Royal Naval Division to the Gulf of Saros, its ships standing off the beaches, its men providing a diversion to keep the binoculars of the Ottoman forces firmly trained upon them – and away from the activities farther south. As if this was not enough, the Allied Commander-in-Chief would also send the French to take the Dardanelles fortress of Kum Kale, providing a hint that maybe the Allies' objectives lay on both sides of the Straits. General d'Amade's task at Kum Kale was not just a demonstration; his men would have to take the forts capable of bombarding the innermost landing beaches.

In reality, it was the beach at Gaba Tepe that held the most tempting opportunities for a commander committed to taking the Peninsula. Here, then, as now, there is a natural route across its girth, leading from its Aegean coast to the Dardanelles themselves, and the village of Maidos. A rush across the Peninsula, taking the village, would mean that the Dardanelles defences could be taken in reverse. Yet, this military approach was so obvious that only the most foolish commander would take his chances here. On either side of the gap, a river valley that stretches across this narrow tract of land, are the steeper hills of the Kilid Bahr Plateau and the foothills of the Sari Bair Range. Strongly defended, the lightly armed attackers would be picked off, the campaign very quickly in tatters. For these reasons, the beach at Gaba Tepe was never really going to be an option for an amphibious landing. However, what if the dash and verve of the Anzac forces could be used against Sari Bair? A major diversionary attack could be enough to hold the Ottomans, and keep open a path into the enemy's rear.

Split into three parallel ridges with access to the commanding summit, named Chunuk Bair, the Anzacs could be landed north of Gaba Tepe and might have a chance of forcing their way to the top of the great mass of the hill, sweeping down its reverse slopes to join with the men of the 29th. In this way, the kill zone that would be the valley across the Peninsula would be avoided, and the town of Maidos, and the Straits' defences, could be taken in reverse. Yet, Hamilton reasoned, if the slopes were to prove too much – or the defences too strong – the Anzacs could be withdrawn and sent south to the jewel in the crown, the beaches and slopes at Helles. Ian Hamilton issued his orders:

General Headquarters
21 April 1915
Soldiers of France and of The King

Before us lies an adventure unprecedented in modern war. Together with our comrades of the Fleet, we are about to force a landing on an open beach in the face of positions which have been vaunted by our enemies as impregnable…

The whole world will be watching your progress. Let us prove ourselves worthy of the great feat of arms entrusted to us.

Ian Hamilton, General

Cape Helles

25 April

Hamilton launches his plan to take the beach at Cape Helles and push through to Achi Baba. Royal Navy bombardment commences a few days before landings.

4am	1st Battalion Lancashire Fusiliers commence approach and landings at W Beach
5am	1-hour naval bombardment, prior to general landings at Cape Helles
5.45am	1st Battalion Kings Own Scottish Borderers, Plymouth Battalion RMLI and single company of 2nd Battalion South Wales Borderers are landed on Y Beach
6am	1st Battalion Royal Dublin Fusiliers approach V Beach with little opposition, but on landing are subject to heavy enemy fire
6.30am	2nd Battalion Royal Fusiliers land at X Beach
7.30am	2nd Battalion South Wales Borderers complete landings at S Beach
8.30am	Despite 70 per cent losses at V Beach, Hunter-Weston orders main force to land; Hamilton intervenes and directs them to W Beach
9am	Lancashire Fusiliers take W Beach
9.30am	Reinforcements land at W Beach
10am	W Beach trenches are captured and beach secured
4pm	Hill 138 is captured with the help of the Worcester Regiment; Hill 114 taken earlier by Royal Fusiliers and Lancashire Fusiliers
4pm	At Y Beach Ottoman reinforcements attack Allied troops
5.40pm	Ottoman counterattack at Y Beach intensifies

26 April

The morning assault at V Beach stalls due to Ottoman bombardment; Lieutenant Colonel Charles Doughty-Wylie rallies attack that carries Hill 141.

| 26 April | 11.30am | Troops at Y Beach are ordered to withdraw in the face of high casualties from Ottoman assault |
| | 3pm | Assault at V Beach is complete |

Cape Helles was always going to be the toughest nut to crack. Closest to the Narrows themselves, and providing access up the low slope of the Kilid Bahr Plateau, if they could be taken, the narrow beaches and steep cliffs would allow the Allies direct access to the top of Achi Baba, just 6 miles away up a low slope. In the days before the landings, the Royal Naval Air Service in their fragile aircraft plied their trade over the top of they hill, plotting the location of trenches, scrutinising the activity below. Obvious to all military commanders, the capture of this otherwise insignificant topographical feature would be a priority. For from here the forts of the Narrows could be taken in reverse, the guns silenced and the minesweepers allowed to go about their business. The fleet could then press on towards the Golden Horn at Constantinople, and shake the very foundation of Ottoman faith in joining the Central Powers – or at least, it was hoped.

This was Hamilton's plan, to be executed at dawn on 25 April 1915. Pinning his hopes on the landings at Cape Helles, Hamilton had as his divisional commander, Major General Sir Aylmer Hunter-Weston, promoted to the job of commanding the division from his original command of the 11th Infantry Brigade on the

HUNTER-WESTON

Major General Aylmer Hunter-Weston, known as Hunter-Bunter due to his brusque attitude, was no stranger to pressing on in the face of adversity (and advice). He was to be withdrawn from Gallipoli due to nervous exhaustion (and sunstroke), but went on to lead the VIII Corps in time for the opening of the Battle of the Somme on 1 July 1916. It would be his corps that would sustain most casualties, with minor gains.

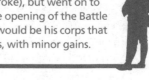

34. Major General Sir Aylmer Hunter-Weston, commanding 29th Division. Hunter-Weston is usually portrayed in a negative light, though some historians have attempted to resuscitate his reputation, with varying success.

Western Front. Hunter-Weston was a controversial figure; his regard for the troops in his command was notoriously low, and his willingness to sustain casualties infamous. In taking the narrow beaches on a defended shore, this could have worked in Hamilton's favour; it would be costly in the later struggles to take the village of Krithia, and the 'heights' of Achi Baba.

The 29th Division landing force consisted of ten battalions in three brigades, with the Plymouth and Anson battalions attached from the Royal Naval Division. The plan involved two waves: a covering force (the 86th Brigade), intended as the assault troops that would take and secure the landing beaches; and the main force following up that would move off the beaches, storming the Ottoman strongholds of Krithia and Achi Baba.

Prior to the landings there was to be a 1-hour naval bombardment at 5am; and there were five separate beaches, dotted around the tip of the Peninsula, which resembles the outstretched palm of a right hand. Y and X beaches (the thumb), were narrow with steep cliffs; in fact, Y Beach had little claim to be a beach at all, narrow and steeply shelving. W and V beaches were points of the fingers, and were the most significant. W is a narrow arc of beach between cliffs; V, a bowl-shaped amphitheatre with cliffs to the west, and a stone fort to the east. Finally, S Beach (the little finger) was just within the entrance to the Dardanelles; it was a wider beach, but one covered by the Ottoman guns on the Asiatic shore.

After much debate between the general staff aboard HMS *Queen Elizabeth* in the days before the landings, it was decided that the initial assaults by the covering force on the beaches would be made from 'tows' of boats, each commanded by a naval officer, and each starting out from a naval warship. This was essential as rather than asking the heavily laden combat troops to climb down the side of transport ships, they would be better off leaping from boats into the surf of the landing beaches. Three warships – HMS *Implacable*, HMS *Euryalus* and HMS *Cornwallis* (and their officers and seamen) – and one 'fleet sweeper' (a former cross-channel cargo boat) were to take an active part in delivering the troops to the beaches. Once the enemy was subdued, it was felt that the main force could land in greater numbers from transports. In all, it was intended that 4,900 men would be landed from open boats. The one major exception to this was the use of a lesson from military history – that of the Trojan Horse.

V Beach

The 270-metre long beach was open to fire from two sides, the cliffs of Cape Helles itself on the left (the site of a naval fortification, Fort Etrugrul (Fort No. 1) and the old fort of Sedd el Bahir (Fort No. 3) on the right, at the very tip of the Narrows. It was an open bowl, heavily defended by trenches that were skilfully dug to contour the open space and maximise the firepower that the Ottoman riflemen (from the 3rd Battalion of the 26th Regiment) would have, pouring Mauser fire down into kill zone on the beach. This would be backed up with what few Maxim machine guns were available, just four, located so as to contribute fire across the beach, cutting down the men brave enough to set foot there.

Here, Commander E. Unwin of HMS *Hussar* suggested the use of a modern-day 'Trojan Horse', that would be able to deliver a larger body of troops with an element of surprise – and in the face of enemy fire. An old coal-carrying craft or 'collier', the

35. The assault on V Beach from the SS River Clyde. *A popular choice for military artists of the day, many of the details are incorrect; what is conveyed is the sheer bravery of those who emerged from its 'sally ports' into a hail of fire.*

SS *River Clyde*, was selected for the task, commanded by Unwin himself. Capable of carrying 2,000 men (two battalions), the ship was modified with two large openings cut in her bows, and fitted with external gangways; these would, it was hoped, be joined to the beach by a tow of three lighters (a type of barge) towed inshore by a flat-bottomed steam hopper (the *Argyll*) normally used to carry dredgings. In this way, the ship would run aground, the lighters placed into position, and the men emerge from what were romantically called 'sally ports'; all the while the Ottoman defenders looking on. It was hoped that the *River Clyde* would give protection to the living (with machine guns fitted in the bows behind sandbags), succour to the wounded, and be a longer term aid in supplying water to the hard-pressed landing force from its condensers. The *River Clyde* would divulge its living cargo to back up the brave men stepping from open boats onto the beach.

First ashore from open boats, at 6am, were men of the 1st Battalion Royal Dublin Fusiliers. As the boats approached, there seemed to be no response from the Ottomans; perhaps the naval bombardment had done its job? The battle-hardened veterans of the 26th Regiment maintained their fire discipline until the boats were beached. Then the firing started; of 700 men of the Dublins, only 300 would survive, pinned down in the crossfire, and sheltering below a 1 metre-high sandbank close to the water's edge.

> Two companies of the Dublins in 'tows' came up… and were met with a terrific rifle and machine gun fire. They were literally slaughtered like rats in a trap.
>
> Captain G.W. Geddes, 1st Royal Munster Fusiliers

Everywhere there were dead and dying men.

To this unedifying sight were added the men from the *River Clyde*. The ship had followed the boats onto the beach, and ran aground near a limestone outcrop that jutted out as a narrow but rocky spit close to the fort of Sedd el Bahir.

> The *River Clyde* came into position off Sedd-el-Bahr in advance of the tows, and, just as the latter reached the shore, Commander Unwin beached his ship also. Whilst the boats and the collier were approaching the landing place the Turks made no sign.
>
> General Sir Ian Hamilton

However, *River Clyde* was too far out for the men to get ashore without drowning in their combat equipment. A complex operation in the first place, the use of the *Argyll* to bring the wooden lighters into place to form a floating jetty also went awry. Commander Unwin, leading Seaman Williams and Lieutenant Drewry would all earn the Victoria Cross, jumping into the sea and physically manhandling the ropes to bring the lighters together to allow the men of the 1st Battalion Royal Munster Fusiliers, and a further company of Royal Dublin Fusiliers, to surge out of the 'sally ports' and down the gangways.

Now came the moment for the *River Clyde* to pour forth her living freight; but grievous delay was caused here by the difficulty of placing the lighters in position… A company of the Munster Fusiliers led the way: but, short as was the distance, few of the men ever reached the farther side of the beach through the hail of bullets which poured down upon them from both flanks and the front.

General Sir Ian Hamilton

Cut down by the Ottoman fire, these men suffered 70 per cent casualties. The lighters were full of dead and wounded, while those able to get ashore joined the others below the sandbank. They would remain in this position until nightfall, the beach not taken until the following day. Yet, perhaps oblivious (or ignorant) of the suffering of his men, Hunter-Weston ordered the main force to land at 8.30am, despite the failure of the covering force to get off the beach; Hamilton

36. An analysis of V Beach. Though built over now, it is still possible to get a sense of the amphitheatre that met the attackers, allowing the Ottomans to pour fire into the bunched men landing from the boats, and the River Clyde. *The existence of machine guns is disputed by some; the effort was no less heroic without them. V Beach cemetery is in the lower ground of the picture.*

had to intervene – the main force would now divert to W Beach. The 1,000 men remaining aboard the *River Clyde*, including the 2nd Battalion Hampshire Regiment under Major Beckwith, waited until nightfall before making another attempt to land.

In the morning of 26 April, the assault at V Beach stalled; Beckwith pressed ahead through the right flank, within the walls of the still defended fort of Sedd el Bahir. Yet the defences at V Beach included at least two strongpoints, wired in and capable of observing and directing fire to the beach. One of these was Hill 141, farther up the slope of the amphitheatre and within the village itself, where there was an old fortification, and which was held in force. Assisting Beckwith, a staff officer, Lieutenant Colonel Charles Doughty-Wylie, organised and led an attack through and on both sides of the village – eventually carrying the fortified position of Hill 141. The assault at V Beach was complete by 3pm, yet Doughty-Wylie would pay for his bravery with his life. He was awarded the Victoria Cross and his grave still marks the spot where he lost his life, now named Doughty-Wylie Hill.

W Beach (Lancashire Landing) and X Beach (Implacable Landing)

If V Beach formed an amphitheatre, then its neighbour to the west, W Beach, was slot-like, its narrow beach spilling out in front of the steep cliffs. Though the beach area is nominally wider than that of V Beach, it is tightly constrained by the cliffs behind it, narrowing to a ravine cut by nature through the layered limestone cliffs that form Cape Helles. Once landed, the attackers would be crowded into this confined space – exit from the beach a dangerous task if the cliffs could not somehow be scaled. The defensive positions put in place by the Ottomans prior to the landings were extensive, with cliff-top fire trenches, barbed wire entanglements on the beach, and, it is argued, at least one machine gun – though modern Turkish historians dispute this. The defenders were a single company from the 3rd Battalion of the 26th Regiment;

able soldiers like their colleagues at V Beach, they again were disciplined, capable of holding their fire until the enemy beached.

At W Beach, there was to be no 'Trojan Horse'. Here men of the 1st Battalion Lancashire Fusiliers (LFs) were to earn their 'six VCs before breakfast'. Transferred to twenty-eight boats from HMS *Euryalus* (and eight from the *Implacable*) at 4am on 25 April 1915, the Lancashires were towed ashore by steam pinnaces; at around 50 yards offshore they were cast off to row in. With barbed wire entanglements down into the sea, the Lancashires had the utmost difficulty getting ashore, especially as the defenders once more held off their fire until it could do the most damage. The battalion War Diary records the stark statement: 'Heavy Casualties'. Leaping from the boats, many were surprised by the deep water; others struggled against the barbed wire entanglements on the beach:

> They [the Ottomans] did not fire until the boats began to ground, and the rifles and machine guns poured into us as we got out of the boats and made for the sandy shore. There was tremendously strong barbed wire where my boat landed. Men were being hit in the boats and as they splashed ashore… There was a man there before me shouting for wire-cutters. I got mine out, but could not make the slightest impression. The front of the wire by now was a thick mass of men, the majority of whom never moved again.
>
> Captain H.R. Clayton, 1st Battalion Lancashire Fusiliers, W Beach

Yet the experienced soldiers of the Lancashire Fusiliers pressed ahead, and some found a way around the headland of Tekke Burnu to the west and forced the defence to crumble. The beach was taken by 9am; reinforcements started landing at 9:30 and by 10am, the lines of trenches had been captured and the beach was secured.

At X Beach, around the headland from W Beach, the 2nd Battalion Royal Fusiliers had landed from HMS *Implacable*'s open boats (X Beach would come to be called 'Implacable Landing', just as W Beach would earn the name 'Lancashire Landing'). Largely unopposed, two companies were ashore by 6.30am without a casualty, the

37. Captain Willis (with stick) leads the 1st Battalion Lancashire Fusiliers through the wire obstacles at W Beach, Lancashire Landing. Willis and five other brave men would earn the Victoria Cross – the famous 'six VCs before breakfast'.

Ottoman defenders retreating in the face of direct bombardment by the *Implacable* and HMS *Dublin*. Here the Fusiliers were to capture an ancient Nordenfeldt 'machine gun'; this is on display outside the Museum of the Royal Fusiliers in the Tower of London. Yet, as the day progressed, there was an Ottoman counterattack that almost drove the Fusiliers back into the sea – before it was checked and the position held, the 1st Battalion Border Regiment and 1st Battalion Royal Inniskilling Fusiliers reinforcing them later that day.

> We got off very lightly while getting ashore; I can only put it down largely to the way our mother-ship [HMS *Implacable*] plastered the beach for us at close range; however we had our bad time later on. About 100 yards from the shore the launches cast us off and we rowed in for all we were worth until the

boats grounded, then jumped into the water, up to our chests in some places, waded ashore and swarmed up the cliff, very straight but, fortunately, soft enough for a good foothold. We then came under fire from both front and flanks.

Lieutenant Colonel Henry Newenham, 2nd Royal Fusiliers, X Beach

Hill 114, a small, defended hill at the top of Tekke Burnu, was taken by a mixed force of Royal Fusiliers and Lancashire Fusiliers. The opposing Hill 138 was a tougher nut to crack, and the Battalion War Diary records heavy fire from this position; it too would be silenced with the help of the Worcester Regiment by 4pm.

The action at W Beach was to capture the imagination of the generals concerned, and six (originally five and a DCM) Victoria Crosses would be awarded for this feat of arms. Ian Hamilton himself would note in his despatches:

So strong, in fact, were the defences of 'W' Beach that the Ottomans may well have considered them impregnable, and it is my firm conviction that no finer feat of arms has ever been achieved by the British Soldier – or any other soldier – than the storming of these beaches from open boats on the morning of 25 April.

General Sir Ian Hamilton, 20 May 1915

Despite witnessing such slaughter, W Beach became one of the main British bases at Helles, occupied until 9 January 1916. The cliffs were terraced, dugouts cut into the limestone of the cliffs, and the beach area converted into a small port with piers built out into the sea.

S Beach

S Beach lay inside the Straits, and was therefore under direct threat from the guns of the Asiatic shore. The beach was within Morto Bay, the eastern headland of which was distinguished by the ruins of what was once referred to as 'de Totts Battery'.

'SIX VCS BEFORE BREAKFAST'

'Six VCs before Breakfast' were eventually awarded to six
men of the 1st Battalion Lancashire Fusiliers who landed
at W Beach at 6am on 25 April. The six men were originally
nominated by Major Bishop, the battalion's commanding
officer, after consulting 'the officers who happened to be
with him at the time and who did not include either of
the officers awarded the Cross'. The recommendation was
endorsed by Hunter-Weston and Hamilton, but was not
carried forward by the War Office. In August, three VCs
were awarded after a second recommendation by Hunter-
Weston, the awards published in the *London Gazette* on
24 August 1915. However, Brigadier Owen Wolley-Dod,
who was a member of Hunter-Weston's general staff
eventually succeeded in having the other three men
awarded the medal, published in the *London Gazette* on
13 March 1917.

Here, men of three companies of the 2nd Battalion South Wales
Borderers were to be towed ashore in strings of six boats by steam
trawlers; intended to arrive simultaneously with the battalions
coming ashore at the other beaches at the tip of Cape Helles,
although this was not to be. With their heavy tow loads, and a
strong current, the trawlers were unable to make headway, and
the landings were not completed until 7.30am.

The experienced Ottoman defenders once more waited until the
British soldiers arrived in their boats at the water's edge; yet the
men of D Company landing close to the cliffs at the west of the
bay, were largely unopposed. They quickly made their way up the
cliffs, and were able to take on the rest of the defenders trying to
pin down the other companies landing on the beach, enfilading
(with guns firing from both directions along their line) their carefully
prepared defensive positions until the Ottomans were finally driven
out, within an hour of landing. Casualties had been relatively light,
at sixty-three men killed, wounded or missing. However, Lieutenant
Colonel Casson of the South Wales Borderers then made a fateful

decision; he entrenched his position and held the line – while around the fortress of Sedd el Bahir, the men of W Beach were still pinned down at the water's edge. Casson was following orders, but something drastic would have to take place if the objective – the village of Krithia that Colonel Matthews RMLI almost visited that same day – was to be taken.

Y Beach

On the face of it, Y Beach was fairly inaccessible, a narrow strip of sand beneath 300ft cliffs close to the opening of Gully Ravine; its inclusion in the landing plans, at the insistence of Ian Hamilton, was simply to provide an opportunity of putting a force ashore in one of the most unlikely, and therefore undefended, spots. Here, 2,000 men from the 1st Battalion Kings Own Scottish Borderers (under Lieutenant Colonel Archibald Koe), the Plymouth Battalion RMLI (under Lieutenant Colonel Godfrey Matthews) and a single company from the 2nd Battalion South Wales Borderers, would all be landed from open boats, by 5.45am – without a single shot being fired in their direction. Yet, for 11 hours after the landing, apart from killing two Ottomans and capturing two others, the men at Y Beach languished. This was not helped by confusion over who was in command. Koe believed he was senior, yet Matthews had been verbally warned that he was commanded by Hunter-Weston.

Colonel Matthews' record was not to be a good one. He did not exploit opportunities; he failed to link up with the Royal Fusiliers at X Beach (who he had been ordered to 'make contact with' – he was happy to leave that at just visual contact); he missed the opportunity to take the Ottoman positions holding up the other battalions at Helles, thereby putting the exercise at risk; and he failed to exploit the open ground in front of him. Despite this, he and his adjutant were to get within 1,500ft of Krithia unchallenged, by taking a simple walk in the spring sun – no other British soldier would get this close until 1919. It was a blatant squandering of chances – destined not to be the last in the Gallipoli campaign.

Left to his own devices, and with little contact with his general officers, Matthews stalled. He entrenched the cliff top and waited; by 4pm, the Ottomans had brought up reinforcements and set to dislodging the invaders from their perches. By 5.40pm, the counterattack had begun in earnest, with attacks continuing into the night. By the early morning panic had started to take hold of the inexperienced and wounded troops still on the beach. Boats were dispatched from HMS *Dublin* in response to a call for help, and men started to re-embark. With almost a third of his men casualties, including the ill-fated Colonel Koe, Matthews ordered withdrawal to the beach, and all were evacuated by 11.30am on 26 April. A magnificent opportunity had been squandered. As the official historian was to remark:

> Favoured by an unopposed landing, and by the absence of any Turks in the neighbourhood for many hours, it is as certain as anything can be in war that a bold advance from Y on the morning of the 25th April must have freed the southern beaches that morning, and ensured a decisive victory for the 29th Division. But apart from its original conception, no other part of the operation was free from calamitous mistakes, and fortune seldom smiles on a force that neglects its opportunities.
>
> Brigadier General C.F. Aspinall-Oglander

Kum Kale

Hamilton lands small French force at Kum Kale and Yeni Shehr as a distraction from the main target of Achi Baba and the Narrows' defences.

25 April		
5.15am	French naval squadron bombards two villages	
c.6am	French commence landings on the beach	
10am	French finally complete landings, after struggling against the Dardanelles currents; they go on to take Kum Kale and a day later Yeni Shehr	

With the landings, came the possibility of the Helles beaches being vulnerable to shellfire from across the Straits; and there were fortifications no more than 5,000 yards away from Sedd el Bahir. To silence any retaliation, and to keep the Ottomans guessing as to the real intentions of the Allies, Hamilton decided to land a small French force at Kum Kale and Yeni Shehr on the Asiatic shore. Though the target was the fortifications there, the long-term plans for General d'Amade was to join the 29th Division in pressing for Achi Baba and the defences of the Narrows.

On the ground, the French commander was Colonel Ruef, and his men the 6th Régiment mixte Coloniale, together with supporting troops. Facing them, some 3 miles away, were two Ottoman regiments of the 3rd Division, commanded by Colonel Nicolai. The French naval squadron opened the engagement at 5.15am on 25 April, with bombardment of the two villages; an hour later the French troops were ordered onto the beaches, which had received no additional defences during the Ottoman preparations for the coming onslaught. Making heavy progress against the fierce currents of the Dardanelles, the French were not able to land much before 10am.

Yet, despite this delay, the French were able to carry Kum Kale, although they were to experience resistance within the village of Yeni Shehr, which was to hold them up all day and into the next. The landings were also to have bizarre twists; several Ottomans surrendered, and others approached the French lines with uncertain intent, leading to the death of one French officer who tried to persuade them to lay down their arms. Others sought the chance to surrender during the 26th – which almost persuaded Hamilton that the French should expand their operations. However, almost was too late, and before he could rescind his earlier intentions, the French were re-embarked as the 26th drew to a close. They would take their place next to the British in Helles, in time for an assault on Achi Baba.

Anzac

Anzacs were to be landed on Z Beach, north of Gaba Tepe with the aim of moving inland and taking the high peak of Hill 971 to command views of the Peninsula and Mal Tepe beyond

25 April		
3.30am	3rd Australian Brigade set off from the battleships to land on the beach
4.30am	3rd Australian Brigade land on the beach, facing small arms fire from the Ottomans
4.45am	Remaining 3rd Australian Brigade land at Z Beach
5.30am	Remaining 1st Australian Division land from transports, causing confusion
9am	Small group of scouts reach high point of 'Scrubby Knoll', but are forced to withdraw
to 4pm	Anzac troops throughout the day fight to hold the high ground on 400 Plateau, but their fragile line is broken by Ottoman counterattack at 4pm
8pm	General Birdwood called to discuss worsening situation with divisional generals; they agree the line must be held and stabilised
27th April	Ottoman counterattack is forced back by naval artillery fire
28th April	Anzacs reinforced by four battalions of Royal Naval Division, three battalions of Royal Marine Light Infantry and Nelson Battalion
1st May	Another Ottoman attack is repulsed and the line is held

The Anzacs were to be landed at the beach (Z Beach) north of Gaba Tepe, facing the formidable, dissected landscape of the Sari Bair Range. The range terminates to the north-west, its steep face created by the actions of fractures in the underlying soils, part of the same fault system that had created the Dardanelles. The underlying rocks were easily eroded with the work of rivers and intermittent rainfall over centuries; this produced an unforgiving landscape. Here, the landscape was covered in low, arid scrub; the soils rough and easily disturbed, and there was little flat ground. The peak of Hill 971 (*Koçacmintepe*) was the highest point on the Peninsula.

Behind Z Beach (soon to be dubbed Brighton Beach after its namesake in Melbourne, Australia), three parallel ridges (first, second and third) seemed to provide the best means of assaulting the peak. If the Anzacs could get ashore in this inhospitable place, then they would be able to clamber up the slopes that led to Second Ridge; moving through the scrub along the ridge, they would be in a position to 'take the high ground' and dominate the ridge top. From here there would be views across Suvla Bay and its plain to the north-west, and back down to the south-east in the direction of Helles.

Z Beach (between Gaba Tepe and Ari Burnu) was to be assaulted by the Anzacs at 1 hour before dawn, in an effort to maximise

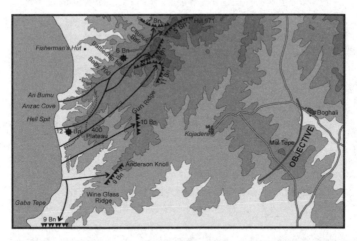

38. Map of the Anzac sector, showing the intended positions of the Australian battalions along the length of Third (Gun) Ridge, with the eventual objective of Mal Tepe, on the Dardanelles. The Second Ridge is indicated by the position of 400 Plateau, the dotted line showing the Anzac perimeter actually achieved; First Ridge is the narrow spur terminating at Anzac Cove.

39. Anzac Cove – this small cove between Ari Burnu and a small headland known to the Australians as Hell Spit was to be the scene of the landings on 25 April. It would soon become a bustling base for the Anzac sector.

surprise, and to try and reach the first positions before daybreak – even if the main body would have to land. Three battalions of the Australian 3rd Brigade (together with supporting troops) would lead the assault under the command of Colonel E.G. Sinclair-MacLagan. Landing at Mudros in early March, these men had undergone a series of training exercises intended to get them ready for seaborne assault from open boats.

The day before the landings, the 1,500 men who were to be the first to land were transferred to three warships (HMS *Triumph*, HMS *Majestic* and HMS *Bacchante*) that would carry them as close inshore as they dared, 2 miles off Gaba Tepe. From here, they would be towed ashore in twelve open boats by steam pinnaces. The remaining waves of the covering force would be landed from seven destroyers, which were to approach close in to the beach. The main force would land from transports.

With the three ridges leading to the summit of the Sair Bair Range as the target, and Second Ridge (later named Bolton's Ridge) just behind the beach, Sinclair-MacLagan was ordered to advance over its slopes, thereby gaining – and holding Third (or later, Gun) Ridge. A mountain artillery unit, the 7th Indian Mountain Artillery Brigade would take up its position on the Second Ridge, on a flat area known as 400 Plateau. Following on closely, the Australian 2nd Brigade would then be in a position to advance up the ridge, taking the nearest summits, Chunuk Bair at the flat plateau top joined by the three ridges, and 'Scrubby Knoll' – a prominent feature on Third Ridge. The main force (consisting of the Australian 1st Brigade) would then arrive to press on to a hill known as Mal Tepe, on the Dardanelles side of the Peninsula – which, it was hoped, would serve as a strongpoint that would help secure the Dardanelles defences. Reinforcements would arrive later in the day in the shape of the New Zealand and Australian Division – (the New Zealand Brigade and the 4th Australian Brigade). In taking the ridge tops, the Anzacs hoped to be able to deny them to the enemy – and ultimately link up with the British advancing from Cape Helles to conquer Maidos and silence the guns.

> The boys swing on their heavy equipment, grasp their rifles, silently make their way on deck and stand in grim black masses. Almost blindly we grope our way to the ladder leading to the huge barge below, which is already half full of silent, grim men, who seem to realise that at last, after eight months of hard, solid training in Australia, Egypt and Lemnos Island, they are now being called to carry out the object of it all.
>
> Private A.R. Perry, 10th Battalion, 3rd Australian Brigade, AIF

Troops of the 3rd Australian Brigade (9th, 10th and 11th battalions) would be first to land; packed into forty-eight open boats they had sat quiet and unmoving for 3 hours before they finally set off, at 3.30am from the battleships HMS *Queen*, HMS *London* and HMS *Prince of Wales*, towed quietly inshore by steam boats commanded by junior naval officers. As the boats approached the shore, they bunched; keeping a wider separation,

ANZAC

The term ANZAC was first used in Egypt, where the Australian and New Zealand Army Corps were in training prior to their deployment to a battlefront. An obvious acronym for the Army Corps, its use is nevertheless credited to Sergeants Little and Millington, who had cut a rubber stamp with the initials 'A & NZAC' for the purpose of registering papers at the corps' headquarters, situated in Shepherd's Hotel, Cairo. When a codename was requested for the corps, a British officer, a Lieutenant White, naturally suggested ANZAC. The acronym soon became shorthand for the Australian and New Zealand soldier – as well as their first place of landing on the Peninsula.

thereby permitting a broader action front, was not an easy task to achieve at night, with few bearings. This meant that the majority of men in the first wave would come ashore on the beach that would soon carry their name – in Anzac Cove.

Gaining the shore at about 4.30am, the Australians struggled up the shingle beach in their combat equipment, loaded with 200 rounds of .303 ammunition. As at Helles, the water was deeper than expected as the soldiers leapt out of the boats; the standard equipment of the infantry soldier heavy enough to prevent them swimming; several must have been dragged under. Ahead of them were the unfamiliar slopes that would lead up to the top of Sari Bair.

The hills, which we could discern through the gloom, were very grim and gaunt, and we felt we had left all protection behind. No sign of life on shore could we see, and we were becoming confident that we should land unawares and surprise the Turks. Suddenly a light flashed ashore... We knew now what to expect. We were about thirty yards away when the pinnace cast off. No sooner were the oars in position, than – bang! From the right came the shrapnel. The Turks on the cliff and in the trenches were pouring forth a murderous fire from rifle and machine gun. Every man not disabled at once jumped overboard. I handed my rifle to a sailor to hold, and went over into the water up to my armpits. Believe me, the noise was beyond imagination; all hell seemed to be let loose. Off went the packs, the steel rang as we fixed bayonets, and forming into some sort of line, up the cliff we rushed regardless of the rifle or machine-gun fire.

Private Fred Fox, 9th Battalion, 3rd Australian Brigade, AIF

The small arms fire was directed at them by around 200 men of the 2/27th Regiment of the Ottoman 9th Division. It was heaviest at the northern part – the promontory known as Ari Burnu, and close to the small ramshackle building known as Fisherman's Hut. For von Sanders, farther up the Peninsula, the landing in the Gaba Tepe area had the look of a feint; he was still committed to the idea that the main landings were at Bulair – after all, there were Allied ships and activity offshore. So, he retained the 5th and 7th Infantry divisions close to the point where the Peninsula narrows, expecting that his 9th and 19th divisions would be more than capable of handling any diversions that might be made there.

However, this was not the only resistance facing the Australians. In front of them were the first slopes that they knew would lead up to the top of the Sari Bair Range. Vegetated with thick scrub that

ANZAC COVE

The Anzacs were to be landed somewhere between Gaba Tepe and Ari Burnu; though the view of some historians is that they landed too far to the north (through the difficulty of steering the boats at night against a current flow). The landing was actually made within the target area, but also a small, steep-sided beach later to be christened Anzac Cove by the troops, a name officially accepted by the Turkish government in 1985.

clawed at their uniforms, Australians of the 9th and 10th battalions struggled to the top of what was later to be called Plugge's Plateau – a small flat-topped extension of what was the First Ridge. They were unable to push on – confronting them was a bald, narrow ridge that the forces of nature had eroded from both sides – the Razor's Edge. This was to be impassable; north of this feature was a forbidding bowl of bare earth that sat at the foot of what the soldiers (in memory of their time in Egypt), would later call 'The Sphinx', a steep-sided cliff, part of Walker's Ridge, that had been created by the erosion of a particularly hard band of rock.

In fact, the geology of the area differed greatly from that at Helles, which in a practical military sense meant that it was a lot more confusing to operate in. Whereas Helles is distinguished by green fields with parallel watercourses that divide up the Peninsula into long slices, the Sari Bair Range was made of drier, more crumbly rocks that break up easily. Devoid of much water, these soils promote the growth of stunted bushes, shrubs and harsh plants, and are easily eroded to form a myriad of gullies, sharp spurs and innumerable dead-ends. For the 11th Battalion men landing north of Ari Burnu, not only would the harsh terrain of the Sphinx and Walker's Ridge be in their way, so would the fire of the defending Ottomans at Fisherman's Hut.

The next wave of men (the remainder of the 9th–11th Battalions, and the complete 12th) came ashore from the boats released by seven destroyers (HMS *Beagle*, *Chelmer*, *Colne*, *Foxhound*, *Ribble*, *Scourge* and *Usk*); ships that were capable of coming much farther inshore than the battleships. Now daylight, the boats were more spread out, delivering men onto a beach that was in the order of 1,500 yards wide, dispersing part of the 11th and 12th battalions north of Ari Burnu, the remainder to the south. By 4.45am, landed into the confusing and inhospitable landscape, easier to defend than attack, were 4,000 men of the Anzac covering force. Under attack from the defenders in the north and facing uncertain terrain in front of them, for the officers in charge of their men it was difficult to know in what direction they should press ahead. They scrambled through the unforgiving terrain towards their target, Hill 971 and 'Baby 700' at the junction of the three main ridges.

The remainder of the Australian 1st Division (the 1st and 2nd brigades) were landing from the transports at 5.30am, the press of men adding to the confusion of those farther up the coast, past Ari Burnu and Walker's Ridge, and close to the small building that became known as 'Fisherman's Hut'. They were once more engaged by the Ottoman defenders – at a high cost to the attackers. These fresh Allied troops were also launching into the attack. The commander of the covering force, Colonel Ewan Sinclair-MacLagan was aware that he had to press on from the beaches to capture the Third Ridge, holding it and forcing on to the high ground – the ultimate prize to be wrested from the Ottomans at all cost. Yet with passing time, the cohesion of his fighting units was breaking down, and it was difficult to identify just who was where, with small groups of men engaged in their own battles with the landscape. It was more realistic to try and concentrate on Second Ridge, securing it from the slopes that lead down to the beach south of Hell Spit, the southern end of Anzac Cove, and along its length until it coalesced with the great mass of summit of the Sari Bair Range. Though some scouts had reached Scrubby Knoll at around 9am, briefly viewing the Narrows in the distance, they soon had to withdraw. No other Anzacs would stand on the knoll during the war.

At Maidos, the Ottoman commanders, Colonel Sami, commanding the 9th Division, and Lieutenant Colonel Mustafa Kemal commander of the 19th, were well aware of the drama unfolding, and from 5am had been committing their troops to the fight. With the 27th Regiment directed to hold Third Ridge by Sami *Bey*, Kemal *Bey* personally led the 57th Regiment to hold Hill 971. The Ottomans were reacting in force, 5,000 troops helping to create a line from Hill 971 that would stop the Anzacs in their tracks – and which would try and drive the invaders back on to the beaches.

With Third Ridge seemingly out of his grasp, Sinclair-MacLagan directed his forces to form strong posts along the edge of Second Ridge; posts that would hold throughout the campaign (soon to

KEMAL AND BABY 700

Lieutenant Colonel Mustafa Kemal is famous for his intervention in the battle for Baby 700 (Hill 261). Observing Ottoman defenders in flight, with no ammunition in their pouches, Kemal ordered his men to fix bayonets and lie down. The effect, immediate, was that the attackers also lay down – and valuable time had been gained. The attack stalled there and then.

become named after their commanders – 'Courtney's', 'Steele's' and 'Quinn's'). Baby 700, sat at the junction of Second Ridge with the main mass of the mountain, would also have to be held. Not for the last time, the deep, scrub-filled gully that divided the First and Second ridges, Monash Gully, would serve as a route towards the apex of the Anzac line. The line would also have to hold across the broader expanse of 400 Plateau, a wider area on Second Ridge covered in dense scrub. (The eastern part of the plateau, soon to be christened 'Lone Pine' after its single pine tree, was to see some of the bloodiest hand-to-hand fighting of the whole campaign, in August). Sinclair-MacLagan was aware of its importance in securing the southern flank of the Anzac line, and as such he intervened to prevent the 2nd Brigade from moving up to their intended position, the high ground of Baby 700; instead he directed it to support the 9th and 10th battalions in stabilising the line across the plateau, digging in where possible. With this decision, Sinclair-MacLagan effectively abandoned Baby 700 and Battleship Hill, but his choices were limited, and loss of 400 Plateau would be disastrous in holding the still precarious line.

As they arrived on the plateau, the men of 2nd Brigade did not dig in, but pressed forward; what followed was a day of intense fighting across the plateau top, the dense scrub adding to the complication. To rise out of the scrub meant inviting intense fire from the defenders; shrinking back into it meant it was almost impossible to distinguish friend from foe – and understand where the firing line

40. Steele's Post, one of the precarious posts that held the front at the apex of the Anzac line; perched on the edge of Second Ridge, it was difficult to access and supply. Engineers were to cut tunnels and saps in an effort to link these points with the rest of the line.

was. Casualties were high. Supported by naval gunfire, the Anzacs grimly held on. The southern flank of the line continued to hold.

However, the situation was critical on both sides. The Ottomans were pressurising the Anzacs, and while the southern flank was secure, its northern component, reaching out to the highest peaks, was under direct threat. Using what artillery they had, the Ottomans subjected the Anzacs to a hail of shrapnel; for the Anzacs, other than a few mountain guns, there was little to reply with. Even if field guns could be landed, where could they be sited? Birdwood was to order that no guns should be landed until the front was stabilised. With what tools they had, the Anzacs dug grimly into the scrubby soils to seek shelter.

On Second Ridge, the flat plateau was the scene of fierce fighting within the scrub. Attack and counterattack followed each other over possession of Baby 700. With fresh Ottoman troops arriving, reinforcements in the form of the New Zealand Brigade (from the NZ and Australian Division) were urgently needed, and Sinclair-MacLagan sent them to the aid of the beleaguered men holding

THE LEGEND OF THE 'DIGGER'

The origin of the term 'Digger' for Australian troops has been much disputed. However, the most popular suggestion is that it relates to the Gallipoli campaign, and to General Sir Ian Hamilton's words of encouragement in a footnote to a letter sent to General William Birdwood, on the day of the landings themselves, 25 April 1915: 'P.S. You have got through the difficult business, now you have only to dig, dig, dig, until you are safe.'

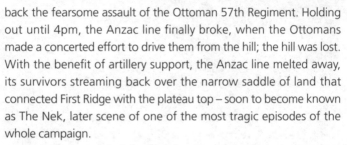

back the fearsome assault of the Ottoman 57th Regiment. Holding out until 4pm, the Anzac line finally broke, when the Ottomans made a concerted effort to drive them from the hill; the hill was lost. With the benefit of artillery support, the Anzac line melted away, its survivors streaming back over the narrow saddle of land that connected First Ridge with the plateau top – soon to become known as The Nek, later scene of one of the most tragic episodes of the whole campaign.

As night descended, both defenders and attackers were in a parlous state. What artillery could be mustered by either side had done its job, and the heavy naval shelling was taking its toll on the Ottoman defenders. After a hard struggle in the frontline, isolated groups of Anzacs were making their way back to the beaches; and there were fears that gaps might appear that just could not be plugged. At 8pm, General Birdwood was called ashore to discuss the situation with the divisional generals, Bridges (commanding 1st Australian Division) and Godley (commanding the NZ and Australian Division). Birdwood faltered; he deferred to Hamilton on HMS *Queen Elizabeth*. Concerned at the level of straggling, he considered that the Anzacs were becoming demoralised. His hastily drafted note to Hamilton ended: 'I know my representation is most serious, but if we are to re-embark it must be done at once'. Finally receiving the unaddressed message 3 hours later, Hamilton sought the advice of his naval commanders – there could be no night evacuation.

The Battlefield: What Actually Happened?

The Commander-in-Chief was to instruct Birdwood that the Anzac line must hold firm. The legend of the 'Digger' was born.

With the Anzac commanders clear that they were to stay put, the front was stabilised, the men suffering an uneasy night. With troops mixed in the confusion, it was difficult to be precise as to where an individual battalion might be located.

> The broken ground, the thick scrub... the headlong valour of scattered groups of the men who had pressed far further into the peninsula than had been intended – all these led to confusion and mixing up of units. Eventually the mixed crowd of fighting men... solidified into a semicircular position.
>
> General Sir Ian Hamilton

The line was held in an arc rising from the beach along Second Ridge (Bolton's Ridge, leading to 400 Plateau) through the isolated posts (Steele's, Courtney's and Quinn's) to the head of Monash Gully; from there it descended down to the sea on the other side of the Sphinx, along Walker's Ridge. It was like a gigantic bite out of an unappetising apple, with a frontline of just less than 1½ miles, its greatest penetration was no more than a mile. Having landed and dug-in, the Anzacs were now told to wait – the main theatre of Helles was to take centre stage. In total, 15,000 Anzac troops had landed; but there were 2,000 dead and wounded, the living crowded into open boats waiting to be re-embarked. They would have a long wait as the medical services struggled with the crush.

The Ottomans had suffered too; six battalions had been engaged, and the three battalions of the 57th Regiment had been almost wiped out in counterattacks at Baby 700. The 27th Regiment was in a similarly parlous state, and the Arabian 77th Regiment had faltered in the face of severe opposition. However, Mustafa Kemal's men had held the invaders; occupying the ridge tops they had effectively corralled the Anzacs into a small area, always facing upwards, their backs to the sea. With reinforcements of two additional regiments (33rd and 62nd), together with his reserves (72nd) Kemal planned to destroy the grim foothold the Australians and New Zealanders had carved for themselves, and to do so before fresh troops could arrive. His orders read:

Of the forces which the enemy brought in his ships only a remnant is left. I presume he intends to bring others. Therefore we must drive those now in front of us into the sea… I do not expect that any of us would not rather die than repeat the shameful story of the Balkan War.

Lieutenant Colonel Mustafa Kemal

Yet Kemal's counterattack on 27 April faltered in the face of the tenacity of the defenders, and the crushing weight of the naval artillery fire. Advancing in massed formation at the apex of the Anzac line, the Ottomans were devastated by the watching guns of the navy with HMS *Queen Elizabeth* delivering five 15in. shells into the crush of men; elsewhere, the now-consolidated lines of the Anzacs, and the inhospitable terrain, destroyed the Ottoman advance. On 28 April the Anzacs were reinforced by the arrival of four battalions of the Royal Naval Division, three battalions of Royal Marine Light Infantry (Chatham, Portsmouth and Deal) and the Nelson Battalion made up of Royal Naval reservists, who were sent along the Second Ridge to relieve the Australian 1st and 3rd brigades. These men would bear the brunt of another attack by Kemal's men on 1 May; but the line would hold. The Anzacs and RND would push back a day later, in an attempt to capture Baby 700; this would also be a debacle. For the time being, the positions were fixed; the front would now switch to the defensive as the focus was on Helles.

The Australian and New Zealand Army Corps… at this stage of the operations was, first, to keep open a door leading to the vitals of the Turkish position; secondly, to hold up as large a body as possible of the enemy in front of them, so as to lessen the strain at Cape Helles.

General Sir Ian Hamilton

The Battles for Krithia

Cape Helles was always the main target; here was the prize of direct access to the Narrows, and the anticipated prize of the Straits' defences. With the Anzac line stabilised, the pressure had to be on capturing the hill fort of Achi Baba, and the small village of Krithia that was standing in the way of the Allied army and its prize. An objective for the first day of the landings, and apart from Colonel Matthews' stroll from Y Beach, it was evident to the British that taking the prominent hill and its village would be no mean feat. Additionally, complicating this was the fact that the delays in taking and consolidating the main beaches at Helles had also contributed to the delay in landing men and materiel to support the operation. The French were to arrive to take over the right of the line.

After the struggles on V Beach and the trials experienced at the toe of Cape Helles during the landings, the evening of 26 May was relatively quiet. Unknown to the British at the time, the Ottomans had withdrawn from defending the beach positions; they had lost some 1,900 casualties during the hard-fought battles of the beaches. There were five battalions left to defend the sector: the 2/26th and 3/26th Regiments, and three battalions of the 27th Regiment. These men withdrew to a line in front of Krithia, crossing the Peninsula; this would be easier to defend, and would be supported by four field artillery batteries which took up position to the east of the Peninsula, at Kereves Dere, one of the four dry watercourses that dissect the low sloping plain of Cape Helles, rising up to Achi Baba by degree. These watercourses would have a dramatic effect on the prosecution of battle in the Helles sector, dividing up the Helles Plain into what were termed 'spurs', narrow tracks of land, largely bare and cultivated between the deeper valleys. From the Aegean to the Straits these would be Gully Spur, Fir Tree Spur, Krithia Spur and Kereves Spur; all would feature largely in the battles to come for the control of the village of Krithia.

First Battle of Krithia

28 April	French 175th Brigade, British 87th and 88th brigades deployed in a plan to capture village of Krithia with ultimate goal of the fortress at Achi Baba	
	8am	29th Division begin to advance, hampered by the terrain
	6pm	Advance is called off; no ground is gained
1 May	Ottomans launch night attack	
	10pm	Ottoman artillery bombardment launches attack. Ottoman troops attack along the British line
	5am	French repulse the Ottomans; no ground is gained; further Ottoman night attack the following night also ends in failure

Unsure of the actual position of the Ottoman lines, the British and French troops advanced up to a straight line that ran across the Peninsula from the relatively broad expanse of Morto Bay (the scene of the landing at S Beach, and a new theatre of operations for the French) to the beach that marked the entrance to a deep and inhospitable terrain feature that tracked north-eastwards up the Peninsula, parallel to the three other dry valleys that denoted the rise of the land up to Achi Baba.

Major General Hunter-Weston was in charge of an operation, which deployed the 29th Division and the French in a major battle that was intended to bring the Allies that much closer to their prize. Instead of a continuous advance on a broad front, he envisaged a wheeling movement, the French 175th Brigade executing a complex right-angled movement, their right flank stuck to the coast, while the British 87th and 88th brigades advanced to capture Krithia. The finish line would be anchored to the high ground parallel to the Kereves Dere in the east, and would present an almost north–south line from which the assault on Achi Baba could lead. That was the plan; it would be executed on 28 April; Hunter-Weston had, however, singularly failed to communicate it with sufficient clarity to his commanders, the text of his orders was confusing and unclear.

Jumping off in broad daylight at 8am, and supported by just twenty field guns, and naval gunfire that could only deliver high explosive shells, the 29th Division tried its best to advance according to instructions. The valleys broke up the advance; the deep cut and wild vegetation of Gully Ravine proved almost insurmountable, with an Ottoman machine gun causing havoc. The Ottoman defenders of the 9th Division (25th and 26th regiments) were proving as tenacious as the ground. The First Battle of Krithia ended in abject failure; called off at 6pm, the attackers ended up in their original start positions. Of 14,000 Allied troops engaged, there would be 3,000 casualties – 2,000 of them from the already hard-pressed 29th Division.

In Constantinople, Enver Pasha was growing impatient. With such a crushing defeat, the Ottomans should surely grasp the chance to drive their invaders into the sea. Von Sanders was in agreement; the Allies were weak, severely depleted from their exertions, and with few reinforcements other than the under-strength Indian Brigade fresh from Egypt, and there was still little in the way of field artillery. Taking the initiative, von Sanders ordered a night attack on 1 May. Commencing with an artillery bombardment at 10pm, the Ottomans attacked with 9,000 men along the length of the British line. The line was severely tested; the Ottomans stove in the front only to be pressed back by those in reserve, and at 5am the French counterattacked, driving the Ottomans back; the Allies had returned to where they started from. Another attack was pressed by the Ottomans the following night; it was to be yet another abject failure.

Second Battle of Krithia

6 May		New offensive is launched to take Krithia
	11am	Allied artillery bombardment has little effect; 400yds ground is gained
7 May		Attack is resumed, with similar consequences
	11.25pm	Hunter-Weston orders attack to be resumed next morning, despite failures of the previous days
8 May	**10.15am**	Meagre artillery bombardment commences
	12 noon	Attack stalls along the line
	5.30pm	Hamilton orders bayonet attack by whole line, which fails with heavy casualties

Hard on the heels of the failure of the first battle, and the Allied defence of their frontline after the night attacks of 1 and 3 May, Hunter-Weston once more planned a resumption of the push for Krithia, and with it the hopes that Achi Baba could be taken. Yet with the Ottomans testing the Allied line, it was obvious that if a new attack was to succeed, the hard-pressed and battle-weary 29th Division would need reinforcement. With the Anzac sector stable and all offensive operations in abeyance, General Birdwood sanctioned the transference of the Australian 2nd and New Zealand Infantry brigades. The Royal Naval Division would also be engaged.

In fact, the matter of reinforcement of the Helles Front had already been a subject of some controversy. Lord Kitchener had got wind of the need for more men on 27 April – but only via a signal sent by the French naval commander Admiral Guépratte to his superiors in Malta. Hamilton, always deferential to the powerful character of the Secretary of State for War, made his request for more men only after the indirect approach of the French admiral. Nevertheless, General Sir John Maxwell, the British Commander in Egypt, was contacted to make another Lancashire unit – this time the 42nd (East Lancashire) Division, Territorial Force (which had been in Egypt since September 1914) – available to Hamilton. The French themselves committed another infantry division (the 156th, under General Bailloud) to the great adventure.

Despite everything they had been through since they stormed the beaches on 25 April, it was the 87th and 88th brigades of the 29th Division who would once more lead the attack. The plan was simple: again there would be a general advance on a broad front that pivoted on the French lines, thereby crossing the Peninsula and all the obstacles it had in the way of terrain; an almost exact repeat of the failed first battle just ten days earlier. It did not bode well that the plans were made even more complicated by the notoriously brusque commander of the 29th Division.

On the left of the line, tackling the complex topography of Gully Ravine, would be the inexperienced 125th Brigade of the 42nd (East Lancashire) Division; the 88th and 87th brigades were in the centre, the French on the right, and the Indian Brigade was held in reserve. With a nominal 105 artillery pieces ashore (including twelve 'heavies'), the prospects for artillery bombardment would have been improved – if there had not been an ongoing shell shortage. Many of the guns just could not be engaged. Facing the Allies in the defence of Krithia were two battalions of the Ottoman 29th Regiment, one of the 56th, two of the 26th and the 15th, supported by seven field artillery batteries and a battery of howitzers. They were well dug-in, with well-positioned machine guns.

The Second Battle of Krithia was to open at 11am on 6 May in broad daylight; Hunter-Weston expected that contact would be maintained between all troops in action, and that by nightfall, Achi Baba would be taken. With poor bombardment, stiff Ottoman resistance with 'hidden' machine guns, and the usual unforgiving terrain – the first day of battle yielded a paltry 400 yards, and was stalemated by mid-afternoon. The attack was resumed on 7 May. After a feeble artillery bombardment, once more the Allies rose up to meet the Ottoman defenders. The result was the same: abject failure. Yet, despite the inability of British and French troops to make progress, Hunter-Weston resolved that there would be

THE SHELL SCANDAL

After a disastrous battle on the Western Front, in May 1915, the 'shell scandal' became front-page news. Colonel Repington reported in *The Times* that the attack at Aubers Ridge had failed though a lack of shells: 'We had not sufficient high explosives to lower the enemy's parapets to the ground... The want of an unlimited supply of high explosives was a fatal bar to our success' (*The Times*, May 1915). The 'Shell Crisis' of 1915 was to bring down the government, and with it the replacement of Winston Churchill as First Lord of the Admiralty. The main proposer of the campaign would hold his seat at the War Council, but not for long.

another day of action. At 11.25pm on 7 May he issued orders that the attack be resumed at 10.30 the next morning, the New Zealand Brigade at the centre, on Krithia Spur. At 10.15am the meagre artillery preparations did their best; by midday the attack had stalled all along the line.

Ian Hamilton had landed earlier that day and had taken up position on Hill 114. Frustrated with successive failure, he ordered a bayonet attack by the whole line at 5.30pm, again preceded by what artillery fire was possible. All were to be involved – even the Australians, who were 1,000 yards behind the line in reserve, and who would have to take their chances on the bare slopes of Krithia Spur. The whole exercise was one of futility; the Australians lost half of their 2,000 men in casualties. The battle was no longer tenable – even Hunter-Weston gave up. Second Krithia was over, at the cost of 6,500 killed, wounded or missing – 30 per cent of the total engaged. The whole purpose of the Gallipoli expedition, that of destroying the enemy's means of preventing the fleet passing on to Constantinople, was no nearer to being resolved. More effort would be required – but not until fresh resources could be mustered.

Third Battle of Krithia

Final attempt to capture the objectives of 25 April

4 June		
11am	Artillery bombardment commences for 15mins, then pausing for 15mins to lure Ottoman troops out of their defences
11.30am	Artillery bombardment ceases and attack commences, with heavy Allied losses
4pm	Hunter-Weston halts attack and orders troops to dig in; 250yds ground gained

Despite his failures to take Krithia, Major General Hunter-Weston was promoted to lieutenant general in late May in order to qualify for command of the growing number of troops that were coming in to bolster the attacking forces at Helles. Now in charge of an Army Corps (the VIII) he had control over the 29th and 42nd (East Lancashire) divisions, as well as the Royal Naval Division and the 29th Indian Brigade. The 29th Division in particular had suffered at both the hands of the Ottomans – and their commander's ill-conceived plans.

> The beautiful battalions of the 25th April are wasted skeletons now; shadows of what they had been.
>
> General Sir Ian Hamilton

In spite of the failure of the broad frontal attacks that were easily disconnected as units fell back or became confused in the complex topography, Hunter-Weston planned for one more 'big push' to resolve the issue once and for all. There was a major difference, however. Trench warfare in all its complexities had landed squarely on the Peninsula, and the attackers were now faced with two strong trenches that created a stop line; the Ottomans were under instruction not to yield any further ground to the invader. With aerial reconnaissance, Hunter-Weston was aware that his much dreamed of plan to pivot his attack north-eastwards was dead in the water; the objectives for his next attack, planned for early June, would simply be to take the trenches in front of him and inch the attack on. The objectives, once to take the forts and guns of the Narrows, had now contracted.

If the Gallipoli campaign now resembled that developing in France and Flanders, it had one major difference. Though there was a growing shell supply scandal on the Western Front – it was becoming even more acute on the Peninsula. With just seventy-eight artillery pieces, mostly field guns (firing shrapnel shells) and some howitzers (firing high explosive), it would be a difficult task indeed to dislodge the Ottomans occupying well-formed trench lines. Attempting to make good the deficiency, the navy deployed its own heavy artillery. However, naval guns fire at a lower trajectory, making the large shells actually of limited use against trench fortifications.

To cap it all, the navy was still holding out hope that there would be a charge on Constantinople, husbanding shell reserves and acting against profligate use in the field. The navy's commitment would be further challenged on 25 May, when German submarines were spotted in the Dardanelles. Offshore from Anzac, HMS *Triumph* was sunk without warning, capsizing in 20 minutes. Vice Admiral de Robeck had already shown himself reluctant to lose any more ships; he would be widely criticised for it. With the world's most powerful battleship HMS *Queen Elizabeth* offshore, there was no way that it could be lost in the Dardanelles. On the same day, in the sight of the soldiers onshore at Gallipoli, the flagship was withdrawn along with the other major battleships. Though HMS *Majestic* was left behind to continue the navy's support; she too would fall victim to a torpedo, sinking in just 15 minutes in full view of the Helles landing beaches. From this point on, the navy's great ships were nowhere to be seen, the army abandoned by the very ships *they* were supposed to be protecting.

The Third Battle of Krithia was to have limited objectives, with a simple advance of the whole line of 800 yards, capturing the Ottoman trenches and then advancing onwards a further 500 yards,

H.M.S. "MAJESTIC" SUNK BY SUBMARINE DURING OPERATIONS AT the DARDANELLES. 27-5-15

41. HMS Majestic, *sunk off Cape Helles. Its sinking hastened the end of the fleet's direct involvement in the Gallipoli campaign.*

digging in for the next push onwards. Hunter-Weston was not to be outdone, however; ever the optimist, he planned for the possibility of breakthrough and advance – once again performing the hopeless wheeling motion of the line that he was so fixated upon. The planning went further. Instead of a desultory 'hope for the best' artillery bombardment of 20 minutes, there would be a feint, a gap of 10 minutes that would, it was hoped, draw the Ottomans (belonging to the 9th and 12th divisions) into their frontline in time for another sharp bombardment, to commence at 11.30am. Finally eight armoured cars (armed with Vickers machine guns) of the Royal Naval Air Service were also at Hunter-Weston's disposal; though how they were supposed to operate on a landscape devoid of roads was anyone's guess. They were to be a pointless distraction.

With the frontline out of touch from the Ottomans, a plan was evolved that would allow an advance by stealth prior to the opening of the offensive; creeping forward on the Ottomans and digging trenches at night. In late May, the 1/5th and 1/6th Manchester Regiment Territorials went into the line, relieving the New Zealanders at Krithia Nullah:

We advanced about 50 yards, half way into no man's land, under a full moon. Our hectic digging with entrenching tools into rock-like earth as we lay flat on the ground was a sporting chance given to the Turk to try a little sniping. By dawn we were out of sight if we knelt down and we did a lot of kneeling that day. We had no time that day to complete communication trenches back to the old front line, so when the counter-attack came, no way of retreat was possible except over the intervening open high ground.

Private Fred T. Wilson 1/6th Manchester Regiment

Fought once again in broad daylight, the Third Battle of Krithia commenced with its planned bombardments lifting at noon. With the Peninsula divided into four 'spurs', the Allied troops were similarly divided between them: the 29th Indian Brigade and 1st Lancashire Fusiliers at Gully Spur (and Gully Ravine); the remaining men of the 29th Division and the 42nd (East Lancashire) Division would attack along Fir Tree Spur; the Royal Naval Division (and its armoured cars) would move along Kanli Dere (Achi Baba Nullah) and Krithia Spur; and finally, once again, the French would be pitted against the heavily fortified Kereves Spur. The battle commenced with varying success, employing the ruse to entice the Ottomans to occupy their frontline trenches:

At 11.00 am the artillery started to fire for quarter of an hour, then paused for another quarter, when the troops in the trenches were supposed to shout and wave bayonets so as to get the Turks into the firing line, then another half-hour's bombardment. All we could see was a line of smoke and dust all across the peninsula where the Turkish trenches were.

Revd O. Creighton, CF, 29th Division, 4 June 1915

Whether it worked is another matter. For the 29th Indian Brigade, the 1/6th Gurkha Rifles advanced along the coast, while the 14th King George's Own Sikhs were to suffer heavily in the depths of

42. A charge reputed to be by the Royal Naval Division during the Third Battle of Krithia; staged or not, it conveys some of the energy of the campaign.

Gully Ravine, with 75 per cent casualties. The 29th Division was held up by stiff Ottoman resistance along Fir Tree Spur, though the Manchester Brigade of the 42nd (East Lancashire) Division had more success on the right. The Royal Naval Division on Krithia Spur would have similar fortunes; the newly arrived Collingwood Battalion would be decimated; it would never reform, and the armoured cars were stopped in their tracks. The RND was back where it started from. The French attack, against fearsome defences, was never to get off the ground.

Hunter-Weston called a halt at 4pm, ordering all troops to dig in – a trench line that was severely tested during an Ottoman attack against the 29th Division on Fir Tree Spur that came close to breaking through. Once again, an all-out assault on Krithia had ground irrevocably to a shuddering halt just 250 yards in front of their starting positions. The concept of frontal assault along the length of the line at Helles was no longer tenable; even Hunter-Weston could see this now.

There would be other attacks at Helles, on 28 June and 12 July, planned by Hunter-Weston and General Gourard. With the benefit of limited frontages and improved concentration of artillery fire they would have a greater degree of success. Conversant with their chances of success, neither would plan to take Krithia – or the Narrows, and would have limited objectives. And Generals Hunter-Weston and Gourard would be sent home from the Dardanelles sick and wounded – the Frenchman ironically losing an arm from one of the guns the invasion was trying to silence. The vision of the Dardanelles was fading from view; the stage would be set for a new chapter, focused on the Anzac sector.

Stalemate: Trench Warfare

The front stabilises into static trench warfare with little ground gained or lost on either side; death and disease are rife

Late May–July		
24 May	Truce to bury the Allied dead
5 June	Churchill emphasises Britain's commitment to the campaign
June–July	Meanwhile the Ottomans reorganise their troops; Allies are reinforced

With the objectives in the Helles sector severely curtailed, and with the onset of trench warfare composed of small-scale, sharp offensives, the war had changed. Now at the height of summer, the sun beat down daily and with the absence of adequate water, hygiene was a real concern, particularly in the Anzac-held area, where the soldiers held grimly on in an extremely inhospitable landscape. Making the best of it, the Australians and New Zealanders fell into a routine that would ensure their part of the line was protected from Ottoman attacks. Everywhere in the frontline the conditions were poor.

> The flies are dreadful, and make life between eleven and four a real burden. We manage to make ourselves fairly comfortable in our bivouacs. My home is a hole in the side of the hill, about 6 feet by 7 feet and 4 feet deep. The sides are built up with sandbags

and the roof consists of three waterproof sheets lashed together.
Biscuit boxes serve as tables, chairs, cupboards and other furniture.
I have my valise to sleep on, and get a daily bath out of a canvas
bucket with a sponge; and at rarer intervals, a dip in the sea.

Brigadier General John Monash, 22 June 1915

The clear, blue sea of the Aegean was tempting, and 'bathing parties' were offered to all, a wonderful respite. Nevertheless, there was no home-leave or passes to visit the nearest town as in France. There was no escape from the Dardanelles other than as sick or wounded, the chances of which increased dramatically as the campaign drew on. Mudros, (the great harbour at Lemnos) the advanced base for the Allies, was the nearest they could hope to get away from frontline life.

Despite the heat, Gallipoli became a miniature and fantastical version of the trench warfare being fought in France. There would be periods of frontline duty and then in reserve; what was different here was that there was nowhere to go. Time spent in reserve meant time closer to the bridgeheads, and time still, in the case of Helles at least, within range of the large guns on the opposite shore of the Dardanelles. 'Asiatic Annie' would drop shells upon the invaders whenever it could.

The work of the enemy shell behind the actual trenches
is peculiarly horrible. Men are struck down suddenly and
unmercifully where there is no heat of battle. A man dies more
easily in the charge. Here he is wounded mortally unloading a
cart, drawing water for his unit, directing a mule convoy. He
may lose a limb or his life when off duty – merely returning from
a bathe or washing his shirt.

Corporal Hector Dinning, Australian ASC

While ostensibly static, the frontline trenches were alive with activity. Trench raiding was common, and the mythology of the campaign now suggests that there were impromptu acts of communication

43. Anzacs at work making jam tin bombs; actually constructed from 18 pounder fuse tins, the bombs included explosive and anti-personnel fragments, such as barbed wire.

– even trade – between the enemies, particularly where the lines, as at Quinn's Post, Anzac, came exceptionally close. The Ottoman barbed wire was thick and unforgiving, and found in profusion.

The paraphernalia of trench warfare was all tried here: sniper scopes, periscopes and homemade 'jam tin' hand grenades (actually made from the tins to hold fuses for 18 pounder field guns, the size of condensed milk tins). The Ottomans, for their part, as the French, used cricket-ball like grenades that seemed to hark back centuries.

At strategic points we installed catapults. They were big wooden Y-shaped affairs mounted on stands. You wound up the elastic as you would a tennis net, with a ratchet and pawl. You held the elastic taut by means of a swivel. Then you lit the fuse of the bomb, put it in and released the swivel by striking it with an entrenching tool helve. Sometimes this failed to release it.

Ordinary Seaman John Cropton, RND

44. Periscope rifle, one of many devices invented in Gallipoli. This allowed sniping during daylight and undercover.

And in another echo of ancient siege warfare, the enemies dug mines beneath each other's lines, seeking out means of planting explosives to blow their opponents to kingdom come – as well as constructing cubbyholes and dugouts for dressing stations, operating theatres, headquarters and other uses. Mines were dug throughout the frontlines, but perhaps none so much as at Quinn's Post, at the head of Monash Gully, the main supply line – described by some as the key position at Anzac:

> Quinn's had a fatal fascination for the Turk. During May the enemy commenced mining in earnest, and this was a serious menace to the safety of the Anzac area. Successful underground operations by the enemy would mean that Quinn's might slide down into Monash Gully, so vigorous countermining was resorted to. The object of this countermining was to get under or near the opponent's drives [tunnels], and destroy them by means of small charges.
>
> Major Fred Waite, NZ Engineers

45. Monash Gully, the main transport corridor into the Anzac sector. At its top lies a water reservoir, dragged into position to supply the thirst of the Anzacs.

In the early days of the campaign, medical facilities had proven inadequate, as the only recourse was to abstract the wounded from the beaches on open boats, with inevitable consequences. Most famous of all would be 'the man and his donkey' at Anzac, John Simpson Kirkpatrick, who would work up and down the lines, moving the sick and wounded to the beach on his donkey. He would become a casualty himself on 19 May. To receive the wounded, field hospitals were set up at Ocean Beach and Helles, and there were hospital ships, conspicuous offshore in their white and green livery, with bright green lights; evacuation to Mudros and then on to Malta or Egypt was the next course of action. Many would not leave. Dysentery and enteric fever were common alongside the usual random casualties of trench warfare. It has been suggested that, at its height, as many as 1,000 sick men were evacuated a day. With plagues of flies and abundant casualties left in no man's land – even with truces like that of 24 May, organised at Anzac to bury the dead left by the Ottoman attacks five days earlier – there would be many opportunities for the noisome insects to do their worst.

> I remember well the first wounded man I saw brought in. We crouched on the firestep to allow the stretcher to get by. Sweat was pouring off our 'D' Company stretcher-bearers as they pushed and heaved the heavy stretcher around the traverse. On the stretcher lay a man in a semi-comatose condition, rolling slightly from side-to-side with the movement of the bearers. He had been shot in the abdomen or groin. The stretcher-bearers had done their best for him. On the glistening flesh and soiled dressings were what appeared to be great bunches of black grapes. An angry buzz rose from the black mass when the stretcher was jolted against a traverse.
>
> Ordinary Seaman John Cropton, RND

The monotony of the food supply would also take its toll. According to a historian of the New Zealanders at Gallipoli, Major Fred Waite, 'Tinned meat, jam and hard biscuits and a mug of tea provided 99 per cent of our meals'.

Transport routes to the beaches were hazardous, especially in the precipitous Anzac sector. Here Monash Gully, leading to

DISEASE

Conditions in the August heat became unbearable. Not only was sunstroke a hazard, but combating disease was a major preoccupation. Dysentery, enteric fever and other afflictions were readily passed on through the plagues of flies that infested the battlefields; they would rise up from the bloated and rotting corpses that littered no man's land, before settling on any food. Lack of water was a problem for hygiene; and unsuitable frontline food – such as corned beef – became liquefied in the summer heat.

46. *Evacuation of sick and wounded on barges. Field hospitals were tightly constrained on Gallipoli, and the hospital ships were overcrowded. Many men had to be shipped out to hospitals as far afield as Egypt and Malta.*

Shrapnel Gully, would be developed as a transport thoroughfare, with pack animals moving to and fro. Most famous would be the Zion Mule Corps – Jewish volunteers raised to serve in the Middle East, whose members were active in the Helles sector. There would be others, particularly on the hazardous trek to the Anzac frontline. In order to combat the water supply issues at Anzac, great iron cisterns were to be dragged into position to store water – that water would then have to be man-handled up to the front. One remains there now, at the head of Monash Gully.

In fact, water supply was a major preoccupation, and engineers did their best to supply it. A groundwater expert was employed to search for water in the limited space that the Allies held; even considering the water that could be obtained from the beach sands that would not be tainted with salt. Where possible wells were dug – like that surviving today at Gully Beach, but everywhere there was thirst.

As to water, that element of itself was responsible for a whole chapter of preparations. An enormous quantity had to be collected secretly, and as secretly stowed away at Anzac, where a high-level reservoir had to be built, having a holding capacity of 30,000 gallons, and fitted out with a regular system of pipes and distribution tanks. A stationary engine was brought over from Egypt to fill that reservoir. Petroleum tins, with a carrying capacity of 80,000 gallons, were got together, and fixed up with handles, etc.

General Sir Ian Hamilton

On the beaches, complex harbours and jetties were constructed, miniature railways transferring materiel to the depots that were stacked in whatever corner was available to the Allies. All was hustle and bustle, and all under constant threat of artillery fire from the shores of the Dardanelles.

For the Ottomans, there was time to wonder just how much longer the invaders would be able to hold on. Would there be a resumption of costly offensives, or would the enemy simply melt away. Winston Churchill's widely reported speech, made on 5 June 1915 in his constituency of Dundee, made it plain for all who wished to listen:

Beyond those few miles of ridge and scrub on which our soldiers, our French comrades, our gallant Australians, and our New Zealand fellow-subjects are now battling, lie the downfall of a hostile empire, the destruction of an enemy's fleet and army, the fall of a world-famous capital, and probably the accession of powerful Allies. The struggle will be heavy, the risks numerous, the losses cruel; but victory when it comes will make amends for all.

Winston Churchill, Dundee, 5 June 1915

Clearly, the Allies were there to win the battle – if they could. After the July attacks at Helles, the Ottomans re-organised their forces in order to meet any further offensive action with renewed vigour. There were new dispositions of the Fifth Army. To protect the Asiatic shore, there were three infantry divisions supported

117

by the Çanakkale *Gendarmerie*. Still expecting further pressure in the Helles sector, there were six divisions, taking their turn in the Helles trenches. In the otherwise stable Anzac sector four divisions were to hold back the Australians, the 5th, 9th, 16th and 19th. Little threat was expected at Suvla Bay – held back from the Straits by the glowering mass of Sari Bair – with just four battalions, two of which were *Gendarmerie*. Still protected were Bulair and the Gulf of Saros, with the 4th Calvary Brigade and the 6th, 7th and 12th divisions of the XVI Army Corps.

With the campaign stalemated, in July, General Hamilton was finally reinforced. Not that he himself had requested this. Hamilton was very much the Edwardian gentleman; well versed in letters and aware of the protocols of the day. It is difficult to understand in hindsight, but Hamilton was reluctant to ask for more men. Maybe it was because he was told not to by the overbearing figure of Kitchener; or maybe he was unsure where those fresh men could be deployed, housed and used.

Yet, Hamilton knew that the 29th Division was a shadow of its former self, and the 42nd Division had been fully engaged in the Helles sector since its arrival in May. On 6 June, a further Territorial division arrived at Helles – the 52nd (Lowland) Division. Below strength, this division had only two brigades – its third had been decimated by a major troop train accident on the Scottish borders. On arrival, the 52nd took its place holding the line in the Helles sector.

Kitchener had been reluctant to commit the 29th Division, but realised now that this was an all or nothing moment. So he sent three of his volunteer 'New Army' divisions to the Peninsula, the 10th, 11th and 13th, and then later loaded two more Territorial divisions, the 53rd and 54th, on the commander. Hamilton seemed unsure of what to do with them. What was clear was that with this number of men, there would need to be a new commander of suitable rank to command an Army Corps. Hamilton wanted either Generals Rawlinson or Byng – both heavily engaged in the war on the Western Front – there was no way he would be granted them. Instead, he had to choose from Lieutenant Generals John Ewart

LIEUTENANT GENERAL STOPFORD

Lieutenant General Sir Fredrick Stopford had served mostly in staff and administrative positions before his appointment, by Kitchener, as Commander of IX Corps, ultimately in charge of the Suvla Bay Landings. His last appointment had been as Officer Commanding London District (held from 1906). Portrayed as fussy and inexperienced, Stopford took little active part in the landings, remaining on board the sloop *Jonquil* during the landings; when he finally did land, he spent more time worrying about his own dugout than driving his men on to capture the heights. Yet, his orders only stated that he should capture the bay as a base for future campaigns – which he did.

and Frederick Stopford; Stopford, more fit, was chosen as being better suited to the environment, though with some reservation. Stopford had never led in the field, but the command of an Army Corps required a senior soldier. Stopford was theoretically senior, yet woefully under prepared for command.

The August Offensives

So, committed to Ian Hamilton in early August was a new Army Corps, under the command of Lieutenant General Sir Frederick Stopford. The new corps comprised three 'New Army' divisions – composed of men who had volunteered for military service at the outbreak of war, they were Kitchener's own creation, and had never been overseas or tried in battle. The 10th (Irish), 11th (Northern) and 13th (Western) divisions were joined by two more Territorial ones – the 53rd (Welsh) and 54th (East Anglian). Finally, there would be dismounted yeomanry, Territorial cavalrymen deprived of their horses, the 2nd Mounted Division.

Hamilton's main concern was where to put the new corps, let alone what he was going to do with them. With so little movement at the front and so little ground taken, there was just no room to accommodate the new forces. Particularly at Helles and Anzac, where squeezing in excess of 50,000 men was just not a practical proposition, even if both fronts could be advanced. Once there, they could be used to resume the trench warfare battles that had been in play since the Ottomans had dug in to prevent the invaders from any further advances. This would be sound, but of limited value. The opportunities to land elsewhere on the Peninsula, at Bulair, or even on the Asiatic shore were similarly restricted – von Sanders had never taken his eyes off this possibility.

Yet, unexploited so far, and relatively undefended, was Suvla Bay and its broad plain beyond. Suvla Bay is distinguished by its expanse of sand arrayed in a broad arc that faces due westwards. The bay was constrained by two headlands: Suvla Point, the seawards expression of the Kiretch Tepe Ridge, in the north; and Nibrunesi Point, and its hill, Lala Baba, in the south. From Nibrunesi Point the beach arced around until it joined seamlessly with North Beach in the Anzac sector. Both inside the bay, and south of Nibrunesi Point, the beach was backed by dunes. Behind Suvla Bay was a salt-rich inland lake, connecting to the sea through The Cut; it was dry in 1915 (but is now kept permanently open to the sea). This would be the very place to land his new corps, being large enough to accommodate the 50,000 men. Though separated from Anzac by the Sari Bair Range, a deep enough penetration into the back-country meant that the Ottomans could be outflanked – if the new divisions were capable of acting quickly.

The bay and the plain behind it were surrounded by high ground, however. The northern boundary to the bay was the Kiretch Tepe Ridge, a sharp, hard-rock ridge feature that tracked back inland; its southern boundary was the steep dissected slopes of the Sari Bair Range that extended through isolated hills – Scimitar, Green and Chocolate – to Lala Baba at the coast. These would have the greatest significance to the landing parties, as each knoll was defended inland; to the east the bay was overlooked by the north–south oriented Anafarta Ridge. The Suvla Plain would certainly accommodate the troops, and could be held as a base for further operations and reinforcement, as the campaign rolled on.

According to Ian Hamilton's last despatch, the August campaign would have three objectives:

1. To break out with a rush from Anzac and cut off the bulk of the Turkish Army from land communication with Constantinople.
2. To gain such a command for my artillery as to cut off the bulk of the Turkish Army from sea traffic with Constantinople or with Asia.
3. Incidentally, to secure Suvla Bay as a winter base for Anzac and all the troops operating in the northern theatre.

General Sir Ian Hamilton

The first day of the combined attacks was fixed for 6 August.

The Suvla Bay Landings

6 August	Troops committed to landings at Suvla to cut Ottomans off from Constantinople and gain Suvla Bay and plain for Allied base	
	Morning	Landings commence
	3am	11th Manchesters carry Ottoman piquet
	2.30pm	31st Brigade and 33rd Brigade move on Kiretch Tepe Ridge and Chocolate Hill, securing it by nightfall
7 August	Plans for attacks on Ottomans in Anafarta Hills brought forward by Hamilton	
	4am	32nd Brigade commence attack, but are repulsed by Ottomans, following attacks are also halted
	9 August	53rd Division land

10 August	54th Division land; Stopford seeks to blame circumstances for failure of attacks, but is hampered by his own indecision
15 August	Stopford relieved from command by Hamilton mid-August onwards – battles of Suvla rage on; attacks launched on Scimitar Hill fail
21 August	Hill 60 is bitterly fought over for eight days, finally carried by Australians with heavy losses; in all little is achieved in the Suvla battles

General Stopford's IX Corps comprised the 10th (Irish) and the 11th divisions; attached to the corps were three other infantry divisions, all granted to Hamilton in a last attempt to force some kind of conclusion to the Gallipoli campaign. Suvla had been chosen for its space, sufficient to accommodate this large body of men. Yet it was too far away from the Narrows to be meaningful in the battle for the Straits, and von Sanders did not consider its defence to be of priority. He still held the view that the narrows at Bulair were under threat. As such, holding the heights of the Anafarta Ridge were three Ottoman battalions under the command of Major Wilhelm Willmer, who was simply tasked with holding up any invasion force for sufficient time to allow reinforcements to arrive.

Stopford's orders were basically to capture the bay in order to make it safe as a British base of operations. He was not instructed to press on if he met no, or light, opposition. His orders gave no direct indication that he was expected to use his men to sweep up the high ground and outflank the Ottomans on top of the Sari Bair Range. Such a move would have been a bold (but entirely sensible) undertaking, and it would have required a general with more 'blood and guts' than Sir Frederick Stopford. Lacking detailed orders to the contrary, and lacking initiative and drive, Stopford felt he had achieved his objectives when his troops got ashore successfully, who commenced making themselves at home. Most subsequent observers, including his contemporaries, have been round in their condemnation of his actions.

47. Suvla Bay from Chunuk Bair; the Ottomans would have been able to observe all that was happening before them. In 1915, the Salt Lake was dry.

Three beaches were selected for the landings: 'B' and 'C' were outside of the bay itself, south of Nibrunesi Point; 'A' Beach was within the bay, north of The Cut. Just behind it was Hill 10, a small knoll. First ashore, on the evening of 6 August, was the 11th Division. The 32nd and 33rd brigades landed at B and C Beaches south of Nibrunesi Point, men and artillery coming ashore on the open beach. Their role was to deploy and guard the right flank of the landings. In the way, and a direct threat to the landings at Nibrunesi Point, was the low cone of Lala Baba; here, as planned, the first of Kitchener's New Army men to see action, the 6th Battalion Yorkshire Regiment (32nd Brigade), were deployed against it, eventually carrying it at the high cost of one-third casualties. Following this, the brigade was to deploy in support of the 34th Brigade in order to capture all remaining prominences on the Suvla Plain: Hill 10, and Chocolate and Green Hills, so named for their dominant soil and vegetation, respectively.

The landings of the 34th Brigade within the bay, at A Beach, were marked by elements of farce. The ships carrying the men to the bay had themselves become lost – the navy had always been

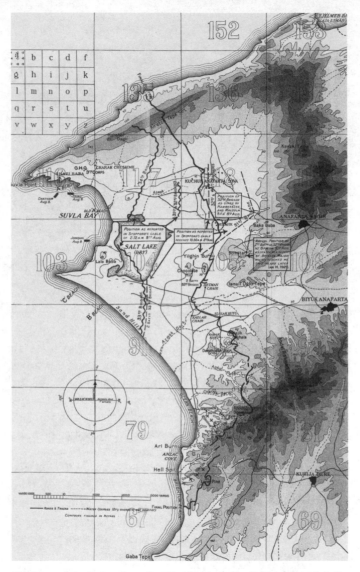

48. Map of Suvla Bay from Ian Hamilton's Gallipoli Diary, *showing the advances made by IX Corps. Hamilton was keen to apportion blame to General Stopford.*

concerned about charts of Suvla Bay. Lighters ran aground on sand bars 50 yards out from the beach; men had to jump into the deep water to get ashore, up to their necks.

> Spellbound, we watched troops leap from the landing lighters into the shallows and wade knee-deep, holding their rifles high, plunging and floundering towards the flat sandy strip in the lee of a 150ft hill [Lala Baba]. We watched them scramble ashore and form up... There they stood in full view of the enemy's observation posts.
>
> Corporal John Hargrave, RAMC, 32nd Field Ambulance

With a defended Hill 10 behind the beach a concern, the 9th Lancashire Fusiliers were to assault it; in the darkness, they were unsure where to go. The 11th Manchesters, landed by lighters from HMS *Grampus*, had greater success, however; they were able to find their way up onto the Kiretch Tepe Ridge, carrying an advanced Ottoman piquet by 3am. And all the while this was developing, lighters plied back and forth to the beaches, repeating the mistakes, but depositing their loads wherever possible. All the troops became hopelessly intermixed, targets for sniper fire for the Ottomans who were scattered about the plain, and were constantly harried by artillery fire.

Stopford decided that two of the 10th Division's brigades would come ashore at A Beach in order to assist in the assault of the minor topographical features dotted about the Suvla Plain. Yet

SNIPERS

The Ottomans were skilled and determined snipers. There are many contemporary reports of snipers caught (or killed) wearing 'suits' of camouflage – covering themselves with green paint and attaching foliage to their uniforms. Snipers added greatly to the random death toll amongst the Allies at Gallipoli.

49. A sniper is captured by the Anzacs. Snipers were active across the campaign and went to great lengths to disguise themselves with foliage and green paint.

following the landing difficulties of the 34th Brigade, A Beach was deemed a failure as a landing site; the 31st Brigade and two battalions of the 30th Brigade would be redeployed to C Beach. Despite this, two battalions, and the General Commanding 10th Division, would still be landed at A Beach. Nevertheless, the split 30th Brigade moved on the Kiretch Tepe Ridge at 2.30pm, while the 31st Brigade (10th Division) and 33rd Brigade (11th) moved on Chocolate Hill, in the southern extent of the plain, storming it and securing it by nightfall. Other than this, by the evening of 7 August, there had been little attempt to move inland. Confusion reigned, and operational inertia set in. All the while, the Ottomans were making their way to the bay. Willmer had carried out his objectives. And there would be no concerted effort to force the situation on the 8th; the newly arrived divisions would simply 'consolidate' what little ground they had taken.

The Battlefield: What Actually Happened?

With time running out, and spurred on by a frustrated Ian Hamilton, watching the landings with dismay offshore, Stopford finally made the decision to dislodge the now growing Ottoman threat from the Anafarta Hills to the east, planned for the early morning of 9 August. For Hamilton, this was too late; and the Ottomans were now present in force on the hills. He insisted that the 32nd Brigade attack as soon as it was able – at 4am. It was soon stopped in its tracks by the Ottoman defenders; the main attack of the 33rd Brigade would fare no better. The offensive stalled. Ironically, Scimitar Hill had been abandoned in order to make the attack – it would never be captured again.

In the August heat, many of the newly arrived men were suffering terribly from the sun and there was inadequate water. This was in spite of the fact that special water lighters had been brought ashore – yet there was no way of discharging their cargo so that it could be used to fill the thirsty men's water bottles. Something had gone dramatically wrong with the elaborate plans to deal with the water issue.

> We were in extraordinarily difficult country, and whatever we needed in the way of food and drink we had to carry with us – even the water. Every drop of water we needed had to be fetched from the shore.
>
> Trooper F. Potts VC, 1st Berkshire Yeomanry

Scimitar Hill was to be the scene of much of the remaining fighting in Suvla Bay. It was strongly opposed by the Ottoman 12th Division and the 7th Division on the Ottoman left, adjacent to Hill 60, a pivotal point at the junction of the Suvla and Anzac sectors. The fighting was intense; Mustafa Kemal, placed in charge of the defence of Suvla and Anzac, was to order the Ottomans to entrench. In the blazing heat of August, the scrub was tinder-dry and the gunfire was so intense it set the undergrowth ablaze. Many of the wounded were incinerated where they lay. With the fighting still raging, the 53rd Division landed on 9 August and the 54th Division on 10 August; the 53rd would be put straight into the line, the 54th held back as corps' reserve. However, the Ottomans were now reinforced to the same strength, and the Allies were badly mauled in the continuing fight for the hill.

In a letter to Hamilton on 10 August, Stopford sought to lay blame for lack of progress. He blamed the lack of water in the bay (the best-served part of the Peninsula for ground water). He blamed the lack of training of the 10th Division. He blamed the lack of artillery. In fact he repeatedly sought to blame anyone else he could for his own inadequacies. Yet, repeatedly pressed by Hamilton to take the offensive, the commander of IX Corps vacillated. Stopford would be relieved from command by Hamilton on 15 August; his divisional generals fell like a house of cards alongside him. Despatched from France to command the IX Corps was Sir Julian Byng. The battles at Suvla would rage on, with limited purpose, and without Stopford, into August.

This last hurrah required the capture of some high ground at the margins of the Suvla sector: Scimitar Hill and the 'W' Hills, as well as Hill 60 from the new Anzac sector. The 29th Division from Helles was once again used to stiffen the assault; it was to attack Scimitar Hill while the 11th Division was to take the W Hills on the south of the Anafarta Spur. In reserve was the dismounted yeomanry of the 2nd Mounted Division. The attackers were soon driven off;

50. The 2nd Mounted Division advance in open formation across the Salt Lake during the assault on Scimitar Hill, 21 August 1915.

the 2nd Mounted Division joined the attack, famously marching in extended formation across the Salt Lake, under fire the whole way. It too would be checked by the Ottomans, as would the 11th Division, assaulting the W Hills. In the Anzac sector, Hill 60 had been largely unoccupied, save for some Australian scouts; assaulted on 21 August, as the last gasp in this sector, the Battle of Hill 60 would last eight days. The hill would be carried by the Anzacs – but at the cost of 6,500 casualties. These battles would all have limited purpose; the fight fizzled out as the defenders on both sides settled down for the coming months, exhausted and preparing for winter.

The Battle for Sari Bair

30 May

Birdwood first unveiled plans to capture the initial objectives, including the Sari Bair Range

6 August

Birdwood's plans for a final assault are launched with diversion at the Vineyard and Lone Pine

2.30pm	Artillery bombardment commences for 2½ hours in area known as the Vineyard to create a diversion from main assault
5pm	Allied troops move to attack at the Vineyard sector; the attack achieved nothing and dragged on to 13 August
5.30pm	Attack at Lone Pine launched by Australian 1st Division, following lifting artillery bombardment; battle raged for three days, Ottoman trenches captured but ultimately failed to distract Ottomans from main assault
Night	Main assault commences: Monash's troops get into difficulties and 4th Brigade halts for the night
6pm	1/6th Gurkha Rifles halt within 200ft of their objective, Hill Q

7 August

Dawn: New Zealanders reach Rhododendron Ridge on the path to Chunuk Bair, other units are lost; Johnston waits for reinforcements

7 August	4.30am	The Light Horse move to attack the Nek, despite not having the support of the waiting New Zealanders; the Ottomans inflict severe casualties
	5am	Gurkhas assault Hill Q, but falter due to lack of support
8 August	3am	New Zealanders are reinforced; Wellington and the Glosters take peak of Chunuk Bair
	5am	Ottomans counterattack at Chunuk Bair, inflicting heavy losses on the New Zealanders and New Army units
	9 August	Allied troops under Baldwin assault Hill Q, but are driven off by their own naval bombardment
	10 August, 4.30am	Kemal leads a fresh Ottoman counterattack on Chunuk Bair, overwhelming the Allied forces; the Ottomans regain Hill Q and Chunuk Bair, symbolising the end of the campaign

There was little hope that the plans to capture Achi Baba could be re-ignited, and with the loss of both Generals Hunter-Weston and Gourard, there was no stomach for limited objective offensives. Instead, attention turned back to the Anzac sector, held on the defensive since the Ottoman counteroffensives had been repelled, with great loss of life.

Priorities changed when General Birdwood, commanding the Australian and New Zealand Army Corps came up with a plan that he hoped would break the deadlock at Anzac. The plan went through several iterations – each time revising its objectives in the light of a more realistic assessment of success. On 30 May Birdwood came up with a new plan that presented the view that he could achieve the objectives that had been set on the very first day of the landings, just over a month before: the capture of the heights of the Sair Bair Range, namely, Chunuk Bair, Hill Q and Hill 971 (*Koçacmintepe*). Using the Anzac Corps and the Indian 29th Brigade, Birdwood planned an assault from the eastwards facing slopes of the range, with two columns advancing in darkness to assault the hilltops. These troops would be commanded by Major

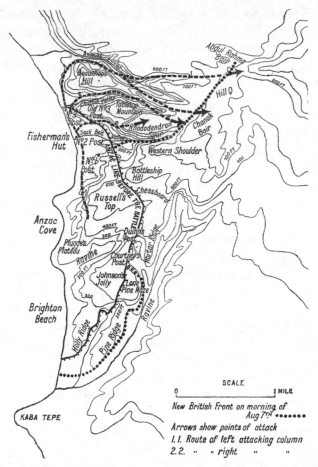

51. Map of the Assault on Sari Bair, showing the movement of the
attacking columns, and the location of Lone Pine. The ill-fated attack at
the Nek was played out in the foothills of Battleship Hill.

General Godley and would initially comprise the 4th Australian
Brigade, the New Zealand Brigade and the 29th Indian Brigade.

In addition to the columns attacking up the lower slopes of Sari
Bair, an attack at the apex of the current line (at the top of Walker's
Ridge on the saddleback feature known as the Nek) would, if it

succeeded, allow the Anzacs to trap the Ottoman defenders in a pincer movement. All was to be expended in this great push, and Birdwood was confident that the attack could work; from here the Allies would command the heights. He hoped that this would offer the chance of siting heavy artillery pieces at this prime location, artillery that would be in a position to shell the Narrows and once more open the possibility of letting the fleet through. A vision that had literally faded from view in all the recent failed Allied offensives, as the objectives contracted.

There were also to be feints that were intended to draw Ottoman attention away from the main assault on the peaks at dawn the next day. The first of these was in the south at Helles, once more the focus of the 88th Brigade of the unfortunate 29th Division, committed to battle at Fir Tree Spur, across the patch of ground known as 'The Vineyard'. As was customary at Helles, the attack was in broad daylight in the late afternoon of 6 August, the assault at 5pm following a 2½ hour bombardment. Like others before it, it was a failure; trenches were taken and lost to the seasoned Ottoman troops. Inexplicably, the battle was rejoined with another bombardment the following day, the 42nd Division taking the brunt. It too was to achieve nothing. The diversion would drag on until 13 August; the Ottomans were aware of both the feint and the likely British intent, and, unconcerned, committed two divisions from Helles to the battlegrounds of Anzac.

Closer to the point of conflict was another diversion at Lone Pine, the distinctive single-pine ridge across from 400 Plateau, along Second Ridge. The intention here was an all-out assault to distract the Ottomans, while the British were similarly engaged in the south. Yet, at Lone Pine, trench warfare had been developed to a high science. The Ottomans had created a formidable fortification, their trenches reinforced and roofed with timber baulks to prevent losses by shell and grenade. Like the battles at the Vineyard, Lone Pine has become a microcosm of the whole Gallipoli campaign at Anzac; hard-fought, but ultimately futile. So, on 6 August, at 5.30pm the attack was launched by the Australian

52. *Men of the 1st Australian Division in captured trenches at Lone Pine; covered with logs, the fighting below ground was fierce and frenzied.*

1st Division, following an artillery bombardment in 'lifts', the line of exploding shells moving progressively inland. Attacking over open ground, they found their route blocked by barbed wire, the roofed trenches with loopholes almost impossible to assault from the front. Not to be outdone, the Australians found their way into the underground maze from the rear, along communication trenches; the resulting hand-to-hand fighting below ground bitter and bloody, its aftermath, a charnel house.

Our casualties in this fighting amounted to 2,000 men, but the Turks themselves acknowledge losses totalling 6,930 in their 16th Division, and of some 5,000 were sustained in a small sector of the Lone Pine trenches. God forbid that I should ever see again such a sight as that which met my eyes when I went up there: Turks and Australians piled four and five deep on one another.

Lieutenant General W. Birdwood, ANZAC

Like the diversion at Helles, this battle was to rage for three days, and though capturing the Ottoman trenches, it failed in its prime purpose. Rather than diverting the attention of the Ottomans at Anzac away from the main assault, it was to attract reinforcement of two regiments from the 9th Division in Helles, and this at a cost of 2,200 Australian casualties, and goodness knows how many Ottomans.

The assault against the peaks of Sari Bair was to be commanded by Major General Godley of the Australian and New Zealand Division. On the night of 6 August, as the two feints were being fought out, the two assaulting columns were to leave the Anzac perimeter, striking out to the west to circle around the westwards facing foothills of the Sari Bair Range. The left-hand column was composed of the Australian 4th Brigade and the 29th Indian Brigade; closer to its target the two brigades would separate to form three assaulting columns, the Australians targeting Hill 971 (*Koçacmintepe*), the Indians Hill Q. The right-hand column was composed of the men of the New Zealand Infantry Brigade, its main focus was to be Chunuk Bair. However, both columns were understrength and included men weakened by dysentery, an inevitable by-product of the summer months' campaigning in Gallipoli.

The two columns moved to the margins of the Anzac perimeter, in the hands of guides who had knowledge of the intricate mass of gullies and ridges caused by the action of wind and water over centuries. Any Ottoman defences soon evaporated, but the left-hand column, commanded by Brigadier General Monash, got into difficulties. Fighting its way through the scrub to a watercourse, the Aghyl Dere, Ottoman resistance stiffened. Exhausted, the 4th Brigade would go no further that night: Hill 971 would have to wait. In fact, the left-hand column would never get close to Hill 971; though resuming the attack approach on the morning of 8 August, there was still confusion about which direction to take. Hill 971 would remain unassaulted. Behind them was the Indian Brigade; slowed up by the tortuous terrain, they too would be dispersed, a long way off their objective.

Only the 1/6th Gurkha Rifles got anywhere near Hill Q, within 200ft of their objective by 6pm. They would make their assault the next morning at 5am, following a naval bombardment. With no other battalions in support – all the others were lost in the gullies – they made a heroic assault on the hill that drove off the Ottomans. Tragically, they would become victims of their own naval support, and with no reserves, they lost their tenuous grip on Hill Q.

The right-hand column of New Zealanders, operating within the more familiar Anzac perimeter, fared a little better – but were still held up by Ottoman resistance. By dawn on 7 August some had reached Rhododendron Ridge, a spur that leads right up to Chunuk Bair; while others were lost in the complex terrain of ridges and gullies. Brigadier General Johnston, commanding the column, waited until he had sufficient men to continue the assault against what was still an unknown level of resistance. This was to prove a costly decision; it was to deeply influence the outcome of the attack by the Light Horse Brigade at the Nek, which was to take place at 4.30am on the 7th.

As the Light Horse were pushing to Baby 700 – the hill that had been the focus of so much attention during the landings – it had been intended that the New Zealanders would be pressing on from their newly captured positions at Chunuk Bair, thereby crushing the Ottoman defenders between them. It was not to be. In the

GALLIPOLI IN FILM

Peter Weir's 1981 film *Gallipoli* famously covered the charge of the Australian Light Horse at the Nek. Controversially, the film linked the order for the second and third waves to continue with the charge in the face of Ottoman machine guns (the artillery barrage having been lifted due to an error in timing) as a 'support' for the British at Suvla Bay – who were famously described as 'drinking tea on the beach'. Yet the Suvla Bay landings had nothing to do with the attack at the Nek.

53. *The assault at the Nek: detail from George Lambert's famous picture,*
The Charge of the 3rd Light Horse Brigade at The Nek *(1924). This charge
was to be the subject of Peter Weir's 1981 film,* Gallipoli.

absence of the New Zealanders, the attack at the Nek went ahead
on the orders of Godley. Rising out of their trenches, the attackers
were armed only with unloaded rifles and bayonets. The Ottomans
wrought havoc with their withering fire, and the three successive
waves of light horsemen were mown down – 378 casualties out
of 600, 230 of them killed. Their bodies would remain on the
battlefield, only to be gathered in after the war was finally ended.

For the New Zealanders on Rhododendron Spur, things were
difficult. The Ottoman defenders were stiffening, the commander

of the 9th Division, Colonel Kannengiesser was in position on the hilltop. Godley issued the terse order: 'Attack at once'. The Auckland Battalion took heavy casualties; while Johnston ordered the Wellington Battalion into position, its commander refused to attack in daylight. Dug in as best they could, the New Zealanders were reinforced by two newly arrived battalions of the 13th (Western) Division, the 7th Gloucestershires and the 8th Welsh. At 3am, the peak of Chunuk Bair was to be taken by the Wellington men, and the Glosters. The navy had played its supporting role – the Ottomans had no way of digging down into what was hard and rocky soil, and were hopelessly exposed. However, this factor would come to count against the Allies.

The new defenders of the peak now found themselves in Ottoman crossfire, from Battleship Hill to the south and from Hill Q to the north – both of which would have been taken by now if things had gone to plan. By 5am, the Ottomans launched a desperate counterattack, reinforced by the 8th Division recently arrived from the Helles front. As the scale of the assault unfolded, von Sanders appointed Mustafa Kemal as commander in charge of the defence of Sari Bair. By that evening, the New Zealanders and New Army men held on grimly, their casualties mounting – the Wellington Battalion would lose 711 out of 760, the New Army battalions suffering similarly.

With Chunuk Bair holding, Hill Q would be assaulted on 9 August by a mixed force, led by Brigadier Baldwin, of four battalions from the 38th, 39th and 40th brigades of the 13th Division, and two battalions from the 29th Brigade of the 10th (Irish) Division. Climbing to a flat area called 'The Farm', they moved up a feature known as Chailak Dere in order to take the assault to Hill Q, while New Zealanders from Chunuk Bair and the Indian Brigade would also attack the hill. Baldwin's men met with stiff opposition. The only force to reach Hill Q was a battalion of Gurkhas, but they would be driven off by their own naval artillery fire, delivered from the newly arrived 'monitors' (gunships sent out to replace the capital ships) and the ageing battleship HMS *Bacchante*.

137

On the morning of 10 August Mustafa Kemal led an overwhelming Ottoman counterattack on Chunuk Bair at 4.30am, narrowly avoiding being wounded. Turkish historian Kenan Çelik has described the action:

> When Mustafa Kemal gave the signal, 5,000 men in 22 lines charged on the New Zealanders and the British at Chunuk Bair. One second later there was only one sound – 'Allah … Allah … Allah.' The British did not have time to fire and all the men in the front-line trenches were bayoneted. The British troops were wildly scattered. In four hours' time, the 23rd and 24th Regiments regained the lines at Chunuk Bair. The 28th Regiment regained Pinnacle (the highest point on Rhododendron Ridge). Just after the Turks regained Chunuk Bair, the Navy and artillery began firing. Hell let loose. Iron rained from the skies over the Turks. Everybody accepted their fate. All around people were killed and wounded. While Mustafa Kemal watched the fighting, a piece of shrapnel hit his pocket watch. The watch was broken but protected his life. He had a bruise on his chest, but nothing else. He was destined to save the country.
>
> Kenan Çelik

The exhausted New Zealanders had been relieved by the 6th Loyal North Lancashires, who had arrived at 10pm (a second battalion, the 10th Wiltshires, had not yet arrived). The force of the Ottoman attack was to prove too much; breaking over the British battalions and sweeping them down the slope into the confusion of gullies below. Baldwin's men at the Farm would suffer the impact of the Ottoman charge. Hill Q was no longer occupied and Chunuk Bair, so fleetingly held by the Allies, was now firmly back in Ottoman hands. The struggle for the heights was over; the campaign effectively finished, dead in the dark waters of the Dardanelles Straits.

AFTER THE BATTLE

With the failure of the August offensives, the complete deadlock at Cape Helles, and Suvla Bay now a rather expensive white elephant, questions started to be raised over the future direction of the theatre. At the Dardanelles Committee the campaign had few enthusiasts other than Winston Churchill, who would soon lose his place at the table. Kitchener, who had originally opposed the adventure, had committed further troops but was now looking westwards again, as the fight against Britain's principal enemy, Germany, intensified. Marshal Joffre had proposed a new offensive in Artois; to take its part in the line, the British would be expected to send fresh divisions – including some of the 'New Army', whose first offensive had been in Gallipoli.

From Ian Hamilton's perspective, the campaign looked like it could be won – if only more troops could be committed. The naval commanders, whose ships the whole military effort had been expected to support, now had a burst of energy. With so much Ottoman effort expended on the defence of Sari Bair, Achi Baba and so on, maybe the Straits' defences had been weakened, the guns removed, the minefields abandoned. This was certainly not the case. Hamilton's enthusiasm was not sufficient to carry the argument; and his own position was looking increasing tenuous, weakened by the political intrigues stirred up by journalists Keith Murdoch and Ellis Ashmead-Bartlett.

Ashmead-Bartlett, something of a prima donna, was a war correspondent with a high view of his own grasp of military matters. He was to stoke up the fires that were growing beneath Hamilton's tenuous hold on his command by writing a letter to the Prime Minister condemning Hamilton's decisions. Keith Murdoch was to carry it to London. Murdoch was intercepted in Marseilles, the letter confiscated. He was to write his own version that did little to support Hamilton's case. It propagated tall tales about the morale and respective quality of the British and Anzac troops (tales that are still told today), and about the skill of the commander. The seeds of doubt were well and truly sown; they were not helped by the actions of a member of his own staff, Major Guy Dawnay. Hamilton sent Dawnay to London to argue his case with Kitchener. Dawnay did report; in fact, he presented Kitchener with little choice. Placing any feelings of loyalty he may have had to one side, Dawnay stated bluntly that if any further campaigns were to succeed, the numbers of reinforcements and materiel were way beyond what could possibly be supplied in 1915, even if there was the will to do it. Hamilton was doomed.

The chances of reinforcement were also set back by the news of the commitment of the French to the Salonika Front. With Bulgaria on the verge of siding with the Central Powers – declaring war on the Allies on 15 October 1915 – the war in the Balkans had become much more complicated. With Bulgaria onside, the much dreamed of supply line from Berlin to Constantinople, and beyond, was a greater reality. The Ottomans could be more easily supplied by its strongest allies. It was decided that Britain would join the multinational front in Macedonia facing 'Johnny Bulgar'. The 10th (Irish) Division was removed from Suvla, the French following suit by reducing their commitment at Helles – these divisions would fight the rest of the war in Salonika, a front where hospital cases from disease outnumbered those from battle. One 'sideshow' was swapped for another.

Hamilton's fate was sealed. At the Dardanelles Committee on 14 October, he was recalled to Britain, along with his chief of staff.

Kitchener cabled Hamilton the next day:

> Secret and Personal. It was decided at a War Council held last
> night that although the Government fully appreciate your
> work and the gallant manner in which you have personally
> endeavoured to make the operations a success in spite of the
> great difficulties you have had to contend with, they consider it
> advisable to make a change in command, which will also give
> them an opportunity of seeing you.
>
> Field Marshal Lord Kitchener, 15 October 1915

General Sir John Monro was to take over command, with General
Birdwood holding the position until he arrived. Monro was
commander of the Third Army in France and had a reputation as a
no-nonsense commander. He was instructed by Kitchener to report
directly on the situation in Gallipoli. He was asked to advise whether
it was possible to break the deadlock (and how this could be carried
out), or whether it was best to evacuate the Peninsula, calculating
the likely losses if this was the course of action recommended.

Monro arrived on 28 October; he at first fudged the issue,
cabling Kitchener with a general assessment of morale. In his own
irascible style, it was then Kitchener who forced a definite decision:
stay or leave. Backed into a corner, Monro had only one option:
leave. With the Ottomans in possession of the high ground, with
well-developed trench fortifications and superior water supply, the
Allies were still in a perilous position. Frontal assaults were the only
option, but frontal assaults had yielded spectacularly poor results
in Gallipoli. If they were to evacuate, they should do it before
winter set in. Monro's blunt assessment was that there would be
up to 40 per cent casualties in any case.

Already a political hot potato, the idea of such high losses was
appalling, given the scale of the casualties so far. With the loss of
face through the defeat of the Allies being potentially catastrophic,
Kitchener was now in a difficult position. Lukewarm towards the
campaign in the first place, he was not going to preside over such

54. All that remains; ration stew (Maconochie) and bully beef tins still litter the dunes at C Beach, Suvla Bay, evidence of the stores left behind during the evacuation.

a serious humiliation. He arrived on 9 November; taken by surprise at the enormity of the task, he agreed to capitulate. The Peninsula should be evacuated, starting with Suvla and Anzac, and then, finally, Cape Helles. Facing little choice, Kitchener's political masters finally agreed a month later.

The Evacuation

The Allies, confronted with the evacuation of fourteen divisions from such small tracts of land – and tracts of land under constant surveillance and in direct contact with the enemy – it seemed inevitable that losses would be high. The weather had turned very much for the worst. No longer was there blistering heat and acute thirst; now the Peninsula became bitingly cold; so cold, in fact, that by late November there were heavy rains, flash floods and even blizzards. These would create extreme misery and even loss of life across the Peninsula. The contrast could not have been more extreme. Monro had originally recommended winter quarters be built on the Peninsula – now it was evident that it was essential to remove the troops as soon as possible.

Despite dire warnings to the contrary, the evacuation would be hailed as one of the greatest feats of any military campaign – the lifting of so many troops up from under the noses of the enemy. Suvla Bay and the Anzac sector were first to be evacuated. Key to the operation's success was the steady removal of troops from the firing line, while all other activity carried on regardless. It was agreed that the level of troops in the frontline area would be thinned to around 20,000 over the ten days prior to evacuation, and all troops were let into the secret on 13 December, the idea being that as many men – and as much as materiel – as possible would be removed from the sector by 18 December. Most of the animals would, however, have to stay behind – the majority shot on the beaches so as not to fall into enemy hands.

With these priorities set, it was essential to get the Ottomans used to a much lower level of activity. There would be prolonged quiet periods; yet, any attempt by the Ottomans to inspect the opposing trenches for signs of activity would be strongly resisted. Gradually the trenches were abandoned, and a whole range of Heath-Robinsonesque contraptions were constructed in order to convince the Ottomans that the Allies were still in position.

With the self-firing rifles sounding in the background, the Anzac sector was abandoned and men made their way down to the beaches in muffled boots; on the night of the 19–20 December the frontlines were thinned until just handfuls of men remained, working their way around the front to give the impression of activity.

A list has been drawn up of the names of each of the last 170 officers and men, showing for each man the exact time that he has to leave the frontline trenches, and exactly what he has to do – whether carry a machine-gun, or its tripod, or its belts, or to throw a bomb, or to start an automatic rifle, or to light a fuse which will blow up a gun-cotton mine, or to complete a previously-barbed wire entanglement on a track which might be used by the enemy.

Brigadier General Sir John Monash, 18 December 1915

By 2.40am, both Anzac and Suvla were abandoned. A final act would be the explosion of underground mines at the Nek; a last defiant gesture that was to be resented by their enemies.

Farther south, the position at Helles was still holding, the last gasp of the British at retaining their most treasured part of the front – the toughest nut to crack, the key to the Dardanelles, and the graveyard of the 29th Division. Yet, by early January, the situation had become untenable. As at Anzac, the frontlines were reduced to a force of some 17,000. The 42nd Division and the French had left in late December; it was the 29th, Royal Naval and 52nd divisions, together with two brigades of the 13th Division (transferred from Suvla), that were to hold the line to the last.

As at Anzac, pre-prepared mines in the Gully Ravine sector would be blown; in response the Ottomans answered with an artillery bombardment that would signal an attack that never came. Both sides, perhaps, weary of the war for the Dardanelles. As at Suvla, animals would be slaughtered, stores torched. In all, some 142,000 men were evacuated from all three sectors.

> The war booty on the south front was also large. There were wagon and artillery parks and whole rows of guns. Piles of ammunition and trench materiel were found. Also here, the tent camps and barracks remained standing, and in part, fully equipped. Many hundreds of horses were killed or poisoned, but a great many horses and mules were also taken and used by the Turkish artillery… The great booty of war material was made available for other Turkish troops… In the next few weeks we saw the Turkish soldier in unbelievable costume made up of all kinds and parts of uniform.
>
> General Liman von Sanders, 1919

The war in the Dardanelles was finally over. The death toll would be enormous:

Ottoman Empire	86,692 dead
Great Britain	21,255 dead
France	9,798 dead
Australia	8,141 dead
New Zealand	2,431 dead
India	1,358 dead
Newfoundland	49 dead

THE LEGACY

The Gallipoli campaign achieved almost nothing but misery. After years of historians considering the great 'what-ifs': if only the fleet had pressed its attacks on 18 March; if only Y and S landing beaches could have been pressed; if only the Anafarta Hills could have been taken while they were undefended – modern writers are round in their condemnation of the Allied failures. Although, perhaps, they should be more generous in their recognition of the strength of the average Ottoman soldier – the very factor that the British had underestimated in planning for the attack in the first place. It is now fashionable that the campaign was doomed from the start and that the great loss of life on both sides was futile.

If there is one thing that all historians can agree upon, it is the lack of preparations. Though the claims of Ian Hamilton and others that the intelligence they had at their fingertips amounted to maps and a few other pieces of information, modern research has proven otherwise. Certainly, the greatest myth, that staff officers were sent to scour the bookshops of Alexandria in an attempt to supplement this meagre and scanty information, has been overblown. However, it is safe to say that the planning for the campaign, thrust upon the naval and military authorities by the enthusiasms of Churchill and others, was inadequate from the start. Whether this planning could have led to success in the theatre, is another matter altogether.

Yet, without the lessons of Gallipoli, there perhaps could not have been Normandy. While the Gallipoli operation plans were hastily cobbled together in a few weeks following the failed naval attack in March 1915, the preparations for D-Day took place over three years; with Winston Churchill in charge of the country, planning for an invasion of France commenced once the German threat of invasion had faded in 1941. So, with the spectre of the Gallipoli failure hanging over the heads of the Allies in 1943–44, it could be argued that the greatest invasion in history might have had a different outcome. Operation Overlord, with Neptune, its naval counterpart, could not have been more different from the Gallipoli landings of 1915.

On 6 June 1944, after years of planning and benefiting from the experience of the earlier landings in North Africa, Sicily and Italy, over 150,000 men landed from more than 4,000 ships along the Normandy coastline. The planning was meticulous, the geographical preparations exemplary; existing maps, postcards and photographs were employed to create maps and reports that were regularly revised and updated from aerial reconnaissance. To combat the vagaries of nature and the determined defence of the Third Reich, legions of 'boffins' turned their hands to everything from artificial harbours to 'mud committees' charged with the safe movement of the tanks. Nothing would be left to chance. Again, the comparison with the Dardanelles could not be more striking.

The Gallipoli campaign was doomed to failure primarily because of a lack of commitment to it from the Allied high commands in London and Paris. Too few men, too little planning, inadequate munitions, and indecisiveness together with woefully inadequate communications ultimately led to the stagnation and defeat of the Allied troops. At the heart of the failure lies an insufficient understanding of the nature of the terrain. Yet, this need not have been so. In the decades before the landings, reports had been compiled by men who knew their business, soldiers and sailors who had cause to consider the possibility of an attacker coming to the hostile shores of the Dardanelles. As is demonstrated by the comparison with D-Day in 1944, planning was everything, and while Hamilton had access to more material than he later admitted, it still was not enough. To cap it all, the landing of men on a hostile shore with the intent of attacking and gaining a peninsula blessed with a terrain that advantaged the defender was a mighty task. Especially given what defenders they were – well disciplined, well armed, well motivated and well led; the Ottomans used all the natural advantages of the Gallipoli Peninsula and sent the Allies back from whence they came. Clearly no military campaign can hope to succeed with such a poor knowledge of the terrain to be fought over.

Those heroes that shed their blood and lost their lives... you are now lying in the soil of a friendly country. Therefore rest in peace. There is no difference between the Johnnies and the Mehmets to us where they lie side by side here in this country of ours... You, the mothers, who sent their sons from far away countries wipe away your tears; your sons are now lying in our bosom and are in peace. After having lost their lives on this land they have become our sons as well.

Mustafa Kemal Atatürk, 1934

ORDERS OF BATTLE

Allied Orders of Battle

1. Battle of the Beaches
(25 April 1915)

*Mediterranean Expeditionary
Force
C-in-C, MEF General Sir
Ian Hamilton*

*29th Division
Lieutenant General A.G.
Hunter-Weston*
86th Brigade
    2nd Royal Fusiliers
    (X Beach)
    1st Lancashire Fusiliers
    (W Beach)
    1st Royal Munster Fusiliers
    (V Beach)
    1st Royal Dublin Fusiliers
    (V Beach)
87th Brigade
    2nd South Wales
    Borderers (S Beach)
    1st King's Own Scottish
    Borderers (KOSB)
    1st Royal Inniskilling
    Fusiliers
    1st Border Regiment

88th Brigade
    4th Worcestershire
    Regiment
    2nd Hampshire Regiment
    1st Essex Regiment
    1st/5th Royal Scots
XV Brigade RHA
XVII Brigade RFA
CXLVII Brigade RFA
460th (Howitzer) Battery RFA
4th (Highland) Mountain Brigade
RGA
90th Heavy Battery RGA
14th Siege Battery RGA
1/2nd London, 1/2nd Lowland
& 1/1st West Riding Field
Companies RE
Divisional Cyclist Company

*Royal Naval Division
Major General A. Paris*
1st (Naval) Brigade
    Drake Battalion
    Nelson Battalion
    Deal Battalion RMLI
2nd (Naval) Brigade
    Howe Battalion
    Hood Battalion

Anson Battalion
3rd (Royal Marine) Brigade
    Chatham Battalion RMLI
    Plymouth Battalion RMLI
    Portsmouth Battalion
    RMLI
Motor Machine Gun Squadron
(RNAS)
1st & 2nd (RND) Field Companies,
RE
Divisional Cyclist Company

*Australian & New Zealand
Army Corps*
*GOC Lieutenant General
Sir William Birdwood*

1st Australian Division
Major General W.T. Bridges
1st Australian Brigade
    1st (NSW) Battalion
    2nd (NSW) Battalion
    3rd (NSW) Battalion
    4th (NSW) Battalion
2nd Australian Brigade
    5th (Victoria) Battalion
    6th (Victoria) Battalion
    7th (Victoria) Battalion
    8th (Victoria) Battalion
3rd Australian Brigade
    9th (Queensland)
    Battalion
    10th (South Australia)
    Battalion
    11th (West Australia)
    Battalion
    12th (South & West
    Australia & Tasmania)
    Battalion
I (NSW) Australian FA Brigade
II (Victoria) Australian FA Brigade
III (Queensland) Australian FA
Brigade
1st–3rd Field Companies,
Australian Engineers

*New Zealand & Australian
Division*
Major General Sir A.J. Godley
New Zealand Brigade
    Auckland Battalion
    Otago Battalion
    Canterbury Battalion
    Wellington Battalion
4th Australian Brigade
    13th (NSW) Battalion
    14th (Victoria) Battalion
    15th (Queensland &
    Tasmania) Battalion
    16th (South & West
    Australia) Battalion
New Zealand Field Artillery
Brigade
New Zealand Field Howitzer
Battery
Field Company New Zealand
Engineers
Corps Troops
    7th Indian Mountain
    Artillery Brigade
    Ceylon Planters Rifle Corps

Corps Expéditionnaire d'Orient
GOC Général d'Amade

1st Division
General Masnou
Metropolitan Brigade
    175th Régiment
    Régiment de marche
    d'Afrique (2 battalions
    Zouave, 1 battalion
    Légion Etrangere)
Colonial Brigade
    4th Colonial Régiment
    (2 battalions Senegalese,
    1 battalion Colonial)
    6th Colonial Regiment
    (2 battalions Senegalese,
    1 battalion Colonial)
6 batteries of artillery (75mm)

2 batteries of artillery (65mm)

2. August Offensives

Mediterranean Expeditionary Force
C-in-C General Sir Ian Hamilton

VIII Corps
Lieutenant General Sir F.J. Davies

29th Division
Major General H. de B. de Lisle
86th Brigade
    2nd Royal Fusiliers
    1st Royal Munster Fusiliers
    1st Lancashire Fusiliers
    1st Royal Dublin Fusiliers
87th Brigade
    2nd South Wales Borderers
    1st Royal Inniskilling Fusiliers
    1st KOSB
    1st Border Regiment
88th Brigade
    4th Worcestershire Regiment
    1st Essex Regiment
    2nd Hampshire Regiment
    1/5th Royal Scots
XV Brigade RHA
XVII Brigade RFA
CXLVII Brigade RFA
460th (Howitzer) Battery RFA
4th (Highland) Mountain Brigade RGA
90th Heavy Battery RGA
14th Siege Battery RGA
1/2nd London, 1/2nd Lowland & 1/1st West Riding Field Companies RE
Divisional Cyclist Company

42nd (East Lancashire) Division
Major General W. Douglas
125th Brigade
    1/5th Lancashire Fusiliers
    1/6th Lancashire Fusiliers
    1/7th Lancashire Fusiliers
    1/8th Lancashire Fusiliers
126th Brigade
    1/4th East Lancashire Regiment
    1/5th East Lancashire Regiment
    1/9th East Lancashire Regiment
    1/10th East Lancashire Regiment
127th Brigade
    1/5th Manchester Regiment
    1/6th Manchester Regiment
    1/7th Manchester Regiment
    1/8th Manchester Regiment
XV Brigade RHA
1/1st, 1/2nd, 1/3rd East Lancashire Brigades RFA
1/4th East Lancashire (Howitzer) Brigade RFA
1/1st, 1/2nd East Lancashire & 1/2nd West Lancashire Field Companies, RE

52nd (Lowland) Division
Major General G.G.A. Egerton
155th Brigade
    1/4th Royal Scots Fusiliers
    1/5th Royal Scots Fusiliers
    1/4th KOSB
    1/5th KOSB
156th Brigade
    1/4th Royal Scots
    1/7th Royal Scots
    1/7th Scottish Rifles
    1/8th Scottish Rifles
157th Brigade
    1/5th Highland Light Infantry (HLI)
    1/6th HLI
    1/7th HLI
    1/8th Argyll & Sutherland Highlanders
1/2nd Lowland Brigade RFA
1/4th Lowland (Howitzer) Brigade RFA
2/1st, 2/2nd Lowland Field

Companies, RE
Divisional Cyclist Company

Royal Naval Division
Major General A. Paris
1st Brigade
    Drake Battalion
    Nelson Battalion
    Hawke Battalion RMLI
    Hood Battalion
2nd Brigade
    No. 1 Battalion RMLI
    No. 2 Battalion RMLI
    Howe Battalion
    Anson Battalion
3rd (RM) Brigade
    Chatham Battalion RMLI
    Portsmouth Battalion
    RMLI
    Plymouth Battalion RMLI
1st, 2nd & 3rd Field Companies
Engineers
Divisional Cyclist Company

IX Corps
Lieutenant General Sir F.W.
Stopford

10th (Irish) Division
Major General Sir B.T. Mahon
29th Brigade
    10th Hampshire Regiment
    6th Royal Irish Rifles
    5th Connaught Rangers
    6th Leinster Regiment
30th Brigade
    6th Royal Muster Fusiliers
    7th Royal Munster
    Fusiliers
    6th Royal Dublin Fusiliers
    7th Royal Dublin Fusiliers
31st Brigade
    5th Royal Inniskilling
    Fusiliers
    6th Royal Innisikilling
    Fusiliers
    5th Royal Irish Fusiliers
    6th Royal Irish Fusiliers
    5th Royal Irish Regiment
    (Pioneers)

LIV, LV, LVI Brigades RFA
LVII (Howitzer) Brigade RFA
65th, 66th, 85th Field Companies
RE
Divisional Cyclist Company

11th (Northern) Division
Major General F. Hammersley
32nd Brigade
    6th West Yorkshire
    Regiment
    6th Yorkshire Regiment
    8th West Riding Regiment
    6th Yorkshire and
    Lancashire Regiment
33rd Brigade
    6th Lincolnshire Regiment
    6th Border Regiment
    7th South Staffordshire
    Regiment
    9th Sherwood Foresters
34th Brigade
    8th Northumberland
    Fusiliers
    9th Lancashire Fusiliers
    5th Dorsetshire Regiment
    11th Manchester
    Regiment
    6th East Yorkshire
    Regiment (Pioneers)
LVIII, LIX, LX Brigades RFA
67th, 68th & 86th Field
Companies RE
Divisional Cyclist Company

13th (Western) Division
Major General F.C. Shaw
38th Brigade
    6th King's Own
    6th East Lancashire
    Regiment
    6th South Lancashire
    Regiment
    6th Loyal North
    Lancashire Regiment
39th Brigade
    9th Royal Warwickshire
    Regiment
    7th Gloucestershire
    Regiment

9th Worcestershire
Regiment
7th North Staffordshire
Regiment
40th Brigade
4th South Wales
Borderers
8th Royal Welsh Fusiliers
8th Cheshire Regiment
5th Wiltshire Regiment
8th Welsh Regiment
(Pioneers)
LXVI, LXVII, LXVIII Brigades RFA
LXIX (Howitzer) Brigade RFA
71st, 72nd & 88th Field
Companies RE
Divisional Cyclist Company

Corps Troops
4th (Highland) Mountain
Battery Brigade RFA
Attached IX Corps

53rd (Welsh) Division
Major General J.E. Lindley
158th Brigade
1/5th Royal Welsh
Fusiliers
1/6th Royal Welsh
Fusiliers
1/7th Royal Welsh
Fusiliers
1/1st Herefordshire
Regiment
159th Brigade
1/4th Cheshire Regiment
1/7th Cheshire Regiment
1/4th Welsh Regiment
1/5th Welsh Regiment
160th Brigade
2/4th Queen's (Royal West
Surrey Regiment)
1/4th Royal Sussex
Regiment
2/4th Royal West Kent
Regiment
2/10th Middlesex
Regiment
8th Welsh Regiment (Pioneers)
1/1st Welsh & 2/1st Cheshire Field

Companies, RE
Divisional Cyclist Company

54th (East Anglian) Division
Major General F.S. Ingelfield
161st Brigade
1/4th Essex Regiment
1/5th Essex Regiment
1/6th Essex Regiment
1/7th Essex Regiment
162nd Brigade
1/5th Bedfordshire
Regiment
1/4th Northamptonshire
Regiment
1/10th London Regiment
1/11th London Regiment
163rd Brigade
1/4th Norfolk Regiment
1/5th Norfolk Regiment
1/5th Suffolk Regiment
1/8th Hampshire Regiment
1/2nd Welsh & 2/1st East Anglian
Field Companies RE
Divisional Cyclist Company

2nd Mounted Division
Major General W.E. Peyton
1st (South Midland) Brigade
1/1st Warwickshire
Yeomanry
1/1st Royal Gloucestershire
Hussars
1/1st Worcestershire
Yeomanry
2nd (South Midland) Brigade
1/1st Royal
Buckinghamshire Hussars
1/1st Dorsetshire
Yeomanry
1/1st Berkshire Yeomanry
3rd (Nottinghamshire & Derby)
Brigade
1/1st Sherwood Rangers
1/1st South Nottingham
Hussars
1/1st Derbyshire Yeomanry
4th (London) Brigade
1/1st County of London
Yeomanry

1/3rd County of London Yeomanry
1/1st City of London Yeomanry
5th Brigade
    1/1st Hertfordshire Yeomanry
    1/2nd County of London Yeomanry (Westminster Dragoons)

Australian & New Zealand Army Corps
Lieutenant General Sir W. Birdwood

1st Australian Division
Major General H.B. Walker
1st Australian Brigade
    1st (NSW) Battalion
    2nd (NSW) Battalion
    3rd (NSW) Battalion
    4th (NSW) Battalion
2nd Australian Brigade
    5th (Victoria) Battalion
    6th (Victoria) Battalion
    7th (Victoria) Battalion
    8th (Victoria) Battalion
3rd Australian Brigade
    9th (Queensland) Battalion
    10th (South Australia) Battalion
    11th (West Australia) Battalion
    12th (South & West Australia and Tasmania) Battalion
I (NSW) FA Brigade
II (Victoria) FA Brigade
III FA Brigade
1st, 2nd, 3rd Field Companies Australian Engineers
4th (Victoria) Light Horse Regiment

New Zealand and Australian Division
Major General Sir A.J. Godley
New Zealand Brigade
    Auckland Battalion
    Canterbury Battalion
    Otago Battalion
    Wellington Battalion
4th Australian Brigade
    13th (NSW) Battalion
    14th (Victoria) Battalion
    15th (Queensland and Tasmania) Battalion
    16th (South and West Australia) Battalion
New Zealand Mounted Rifles Brigade
    Auckland Mounted Rifles
    Canterbury Mounted Rifles
    Wellington Mounted Rifles
1st Australian Light Horse Brigade
    1st (NSW) Regiment
    2nd (Queensland) Regiment
    3rd (South Australia & Tasmania) Regiment
Maori Detachment
I New Zealand FA Brigade
II New Zealand FA Brigade
1st & 2nd Field Companies New Zealand Engineers
New Zealand Field Troop Engineers
Otago Mounted Rifles

2nd Australian Division
Major General J.G. Legge
5th Australian Brigade
    17th (NSW) Battalion
    18th (NSW) Battalion
    19th (NSW) Battalion
    20th (NSW) Battalion
6th Australian Brigade
    21st (Victoria) Battalion
    22nd (Victoria) Battalion
    23rd (Victoria) Battalion
    24th (Victoria) Battalion
7th Australian Brigade
    25th (Queensland) Battalion

26th (Queensland & Tasmania) Battalion
27th (South Australia) Battalion
28th (West Australia) Battalion
4th & 5th Field Companies Australian Engineers
13th (Victoria) Light Horse Regiment

Corps Troops
2nd Australian Light Horse Brigade
    5th (Queensland) Regiment
    6th (NSW) Regiment
    7th (NSW) Regiment
3rd Australian Light Horse Brigade
    8th (Victoria) Regiment
    9th (Victoria & South Australia) Regiment
    10th (West Australia) Regiment
7th Indian Mountain Battery Brigade

Attached New Zealand & Australian Division
Major General H.V. Cox
29th Indian Infantry Brigade
14th Sikhs
1/5th Gurkha Rifles
1/6th Gurkha Rifles
2/10th Gurkha Rifles

Corps Expéditionaire d'Orient
General Bailloud

1st Division
General Brulard
1st Metropolitan Brigade
    175th Regiment
    1st Régiment de marche d'Afrique
2nd Colonial Brigade
    4th Colonial Regiment
    6th Colonial Regiment
6 Artillery Batteries (75mm)
2 Artillery Batteries (65mm)

2nd Division
General Bailloud
3rd Metropolitan Brigade
    176th Regiment
    2nd Régiment de marche d'Afrique
4th Colonial Brigade
    7th Colonial Regiment
    8th Colonial Regiment
9 Artillery batteries (75mm)

Corps Artillery
1 Heavy battery (120mm)
3 Heavy batteries (155mm)
2 Siege guns (240mm)
Battery of naval guns

Ottoman Orders of Battle

1. Battle of the Beaches

Fifth Army
C-in-C General Liman von Sanders

III Corps (Gallipoli Peninsula)
Mehmet Esat Pasha
7th Division (Bulair Lines); Colonel Remsi *Bey*
    19th Regiment
    20th Regiment
    21st Regiment
9th Division; Lieutenant Colonel Kahlil Sami *Bey*
    25th Regiment (Serafim Farm)
    26th Regiment (Cape Helles and Kum Tepe)
    27th Regiment (Anzac and Maidos)
    Broussa Gendarmerie (Suvla Bay)
19th Division (Boghali); Lieutenant Colonel Mustafa Kemal Bey
    57th Regiment
    72nd Regiment
    77th Regiment

Orders of Battle

XV Corps (Asiatic shore)
Colonel Hans Kannengiesser

3rd Division (Troy & Kum Kale);
Colonel Nicolai

11th Division (Ezine & Besika Bay);
Lieutenant Colonel Refet Bey

Dardanelles Fortified Area
Command, Çanakkale
2nd Heavy Artillery Brigade
3rd Heavy Artillery Regiment
4th Heavy Artillery Regiment
5th Heavy Artillery Regiment
Fortress Engineer Company
Engineer Construction Company
Communication Company
Mine Detachment
Searchlight Detachment
(8 searchlights)
Sea Transportation (3 motorboats
with 3 small boats)
1 Aircraft Squadron

2. August Offensives

Fifth Army
C-in-C General Liman von
Sanders

I Corps
2nd Division
3rd Division

II Corps
4th Division
5th Division
6th Division

III Corps
Ehad Pasha
7th Division; Colonel Halil Bey
8th Division; Colonel Hakki
9th Division; Colonel Kannengeisser
16th Division
 47th Regiment
 48th Regiment
 77th Regiment
 125th Regiment
19th Division; Lieutenant Colonel
Mustafa Kemal
 18th Regiment
 27th Regiment
 57th Regiment
 72nd Regiment

IV Corps
10th Division
11th Division
12th Division

V Corps
13th Division
14th Division
15th Division

Dardanelles Fortified Area
Command, Çanakkale
2nd Heavy Artillery Brigade
3rd Heavy Artillery Regiment
4th Heavy Artillery Regiment
5th Heavy Artillery Regiment
Fortress Engineer Company
Engineer Construction Company
Communication Company
Mine Detachment
Searchlight Detachment
(8 searchlights)
Sea Transportation (3 motorboats
with 3 small boats)
1 Aircraft Squadron

FURTHER READING

Gallipoli has received more than its fair amount of books; many of them with the simple title 'Gallipoli'. The most recent have tried to discuss the Ottoman component, but this is a difficult proposition, as not all Ottoman archives are available for use, written in pre-Attaturk Ottoman script. The campaign was short but full of controversy, particularly with regard to the respective roles of the Anzacs and British troops (in part due to the damning view of the British by the Australian historian C.E.W. Bean) – while the French are largely forgotten. The following list is a snapshot of the most accessible, interesting and informative works on the subject.

Adam-Smith, Patsy, *The Anzacs* (Hamish Hamilton, 1978)

Ashmead-Bartlett, Ellis, *Ashmead-Bartlett's Despatches from the Dardanelles* (George Newnes, 1915)

Ashurst, George, *My Bit. A Lancashire Fusilier at War, 1914–1918* (Crowood, 1987)

Aspinall-Oglander, C.F., *Official History: Gallipoli Campaign* (Heinneman, 2 vols, 1929, 1932)

Bean, C.E.W., *The Anzac Book* (Cassell, 1916)

—, *Official History of Australia in the War of 1914–1918: The Story of Anzac* (Angus & Robertson, 2 vols, 1938–42)

Behrend, Arthur, *Make Me a Soldier. A Platoon Commander in Gallipoli* (Eyre & Spottiswoode, 1961)

Birdwood, Field-Marshall Lord, *Khaki and Gown. An Autobiography.* (Ward Lock & Co., 1941)

Burness, Peter, *The Nek* (Kangaroo Press, 1996)

Callwell, C.E., *The Dardanelles* (Constable, 1924)

Çelik, Kenan, and Ceyhan Koc, *The Gallipoli Campaign International Perspectives 85 Years On* (Çanakkale Onsekiz Mart University, 2001)

Cooper, Bryan, *The Tenth (Irish) Division in Gallipoli* (Herbert Jenkins, 1918)

Creighton, O., *With the Twenty-Ninth Division in Gallipoli* (Longmans, Green & Co., 1916)

Carlyon, Les, *Gallipoli* (Pan Macmillan, 2001)

Chambers, Stephen, *Gully Ravine* (Pen & Sword, 2003)

Charles-Roux, Fr., *L'Expédition des Dardanelles au Jour le Jour* (Librairie Armand Colin, 1920)

Further Reading

Chasseaud, Peter, and Peter Doyle, *Grasping Gallipoli. Terrain, Maps and Failure at the Dardanelles* (Spellmount/The History Press, 2006)

Dane, Edmund, *British Campaigns in the Near East* (Hodder & Stoughton, 1918)

Denton, Kit, *Gallipoli. One Long Grave* (Time-Life Australia, 1986)

Fasih, Mehmet, *Gallipoli 1915: Bloody Ridge (Lone Pine) Diary* (Denizler Kitabevi, 2001)

Fewster, Kevin, Vecihi Basarin and Hatice Hürmüz Basarin, *Gallipoli The Turkish Story* (Allen & Unwin, 1985)

Gallishaw, John, *Trenching at Gallipoli* (A.L. Burt, 1916)

Hamilton, Ian, *Ian Hamilton's Despatches from the Dardanelles* (George Newnes, 1917)

—, *Gallipoli Diary* (Arnold, 2 vols, 1920)

Hammerton, John, *The Great War... I Was There!* (Amalgamated Press, 1936)

Hanna, Henry, *The Pals at Suvla Bay* (Ponsonby, 1917)

Hargrave, John, *At Suvla Bay* (Constable, 1916)

—, *The Suvla Bay Landing* (Macdonald, 1964)

Hart, Peter, *Gallipoli* (Profile, 2011)

Haythornwaite, Philip J., *Gallipoli 1915. Frontal Assault on Turkey* (Osprey, 1991)

Hickey, Michael, *Gallipoli* (John Murray, 1995)

James, Robert Rhodes, *Gallipoli* (Batsford, 1965)

King, Jonathan, *Gallipoli: Our Last Man Standing* (John Wiley Australia, 2003)

Lee, John, *A Soldier's Life: General Sir Ian Hamilton 1853–1947* (Macmillan, 2000)

Liddle, Peter, *Men of Gallipoli* (Allen Lane, 1976)

Macleod, Jenny, *Reconsidering Gallipoli* (Manchester University Press, 2004)

Middlebrook, Martin, *The Diaries of Pte. Horace Bruckshaw Royal Marine Light Infantry 1915–1916* (Scolar, 1979)

—, *Your Country Needs You. Expansion of the British Army Infantry Divisions 1914–1918* (Pen and Sword, 2000)

Moorhead, Alan, *Gallipoli* (Hamish Hamilton, 1956)

Moorhouse, Geoffrey, *Hell's Foundations. A Town, Its Myths and Gallipoli* (Hodder & Stoughton, 1992)

Murray, Joseph, *Gallipoli as I Saw It* (William Kimber, 1965)

Nevinson, H.W., *The Dardanelles Campaign* (Nisbet & Co., 1918)

North, John, *Gallipoli, The Fading Vision* (Faber, 1936)

Pugsley, Christopher, *Gallipoli: The New Zealand Story* (Hodder & Stoughton, 1984)

Purdom, C.B., *Everyman at War* (J.M. Dent, 1930)

Prior, Robin, *Gallipoli: The End of the Myth* (Yale University Press, 2009)

Snelling, Stephen, *VCs of the Great War. Gallipoli* (Sutton/The History Press, 1995/2010)

Stanley, Peter, *Quinn's Post* (Allen & Unwin, 2005)

Steel, Nigel, and Peter Hart, *Defeat at Gallipoli* (Macmillan, 1985)

Thomson, Alistair, *Anzac Memories. Living with the Legend* (Oxford University Press, 1994)

Travers, Tim, *Gallipoli 1915* (Tempus/The History Press, 2001)

Tyquin, Michael, *Gallipoli: The Medical War* (New South Wales University Press, 1993)

von Sanders, Liman, *The Dardanelles Campaign* (Translation and Comments by Colnel E.H. Schultz, US Army) (The Engineer School, Virginia, 1931)

Waite, Fred, *The New Zealanders at Gallipoli* (Whitcombe & Tombs, 1921)

Westlake, Ray, *British Regiments at Gallipoli* (Leo Cooper, 1996)

Wilkinson, Norman, *The Dardanelles* (Longmans, Green & Co., 1916)

INDEX

Index